LEADING LIONS

LEADING LIONS

11 Steps to Reaching Your Fullest Potential and Changing the World

Ronnie Doss

LEADING LIONS

Table of Contents

ABOUT THE AUTHOR

Over the past decade, Ronnie Doss has facilitated leadership trainings and seminars in seven different countries around the world. Three years ago, Ronnie was contacted by NASA and asked to begin training leaders of their LION leadership program at Kennedy Space Center in Cape Canaveral, Florida.

In addition to his work with NASA, Ronnie currently works with Fortune 100 companies like American Express, as well as other billion-dollar, private companies such as the Mars Corporation. Whether for major corporations, top universities or non-profit organizations, his message rings very clear; "We don't get what we want, we get what we are committed to." Ronnie lives in Nashville, TN with his wife Jennifer and their two daughters Addison and Kennedy. If you are interested in one of Ronnie's coaching programs or having him speak to your company or team, contact information is listed below.

Ronnie Doss Companies, LLC
website: www.DossTeam.com
email: info@DossTeam.com
phone: 615-881-9431

ACKNOWLEDGEMENTS

To all the amazing leaders at NASA, thank you for giving me the opportunity to train some of the most brilliant people on the planet. Working with you all has enlarged my perspective and increased my confidence. It is an honor to be a part of such a powerful team.

To my wife Jennifer, thank you for loving me so much! You are more than I could have ever hoped and dreamed of. To my daughters Addison and Kennedy, it is an absolute privilege to be your Dad. I love you more and more with each passing day and can't wait to see all that you will become.

To my wonderful family: Mom, Dad, Kaye, Carolyn, Crystal, Regina, Karen, Dave, David, Tarah, Zach, Austin, Joanna, Harrison and Ashlynn. I owe so much of who I have become to all of you. Thank you for the love, support and encouragement that you have given me. I love you all so much!

CHAPTER 1

Prepare for Transition

"Life is pleasant, death is peaceful. It's the transition that is troublesome."

Isaac Asimov

Life is not about what you see; it's about what you *tell* yourself about what you see. It's only when we're willing to admit our own ignorance about what we *think we know* that we can open our minds and begin to change. Since you've picked up this book, the one you are holding right now, I know that staying on the same level that you are on right now is not the ultimate goal for you.

You may want to earn more money, become a better parent, start a business, or maybe you're ready to finally get in shape after years of neglecting your personal health. Whatever it is that you want, you're going to have to fight for it...like a LION.

I don't believe we need more leaders, I simply believe

that we need for more of the leaders we already have, including you and I - to step up and take ownership of our destiny by committing to self-improvement and working to make the world a better place. The good news is that as you work to become a stronger, better version of yourself, the world around you will begin to improve as well.

Challenges are what make life interesting, but overcoming them is what makes life meaningful. You've probably heard the quote, "smooth seas do not make great sailors." I believe it's true! Many people think that the key to a good life is to be comfortable, have stability and be in control. I strongly disagree! In my opinion, having a good life means taking risks, pushing the limits and solving bigger and better problems on a continual basis. LION leaders never run from life's challenges, LION leaders look for challenges, then find ways to create the necessary solutions that will produce positive results.

I believe that the difference between a *good* leader and a *great* leader is in direct proportion to the amount of pain that he or she can tolerate. Long-lasting success is going to mean stress, frustration and even heartache but the payoffs are well worth it every single time. The reality is that no matter what path we choose in life, the path of mediocrity or the path greatness, there will be challenges and obstacles that will appear in our way. We might as well choose the path of greatness! The good news is that the sooner we commit to overcoming the challenges regardless of the circumstances that may appear on our path, the faster we will move toward the achievement of our desired goals.

This book is an overview of concepts and ideas that I have shared in various resources and trainings I have done around the world. To me, choosing to be a LION leader means become the best version of yourself as you work to make the world a better place for everyone. You may not always feel like your best but you can always choose to give your best and that what LION leadership is all about.

How it All Began

Almost 3 years ago I was asked to begin working with NASA on a leadership program called LION. The program was designed to develop leaders within the NASA organization and help them to become more bold, confident and legacy-minded. As you may know, NASA is known for employing some of the most brilliant, out-of-the box thinkers on the planet. Fortunately, that is exactly the type of person that I love to work with.

After my first trips to Kennedy Space Center, I realized that much of what I was sharing with NASA was just as applicable for other types of business leaders like entrepreneurs, athletes, doctors, attorneys or pastors. In actuality I simply realized that the material was great for anyone who was ready to get committed and make progress toward the next level in life. And, that's exactly why I wrote this book. True leaders understand that their achievements aren't meant to just benefit them, they are meant to positively impact the entire world.

My late mentor Mr. Klemmer used to say "Mediocrity is the height of selfishness." It took me a while to understand exactly what he meant but now I know that he was exactly right!

First, living a life of mediocrity means that we are not concerned about the welfare of others. I often speak with people who have developed an "us four and no more" mentality. They believe that taking care of themselves is their only responsibility. When we settle for a life of mediocrity, which represents much less than our fullest potential, we will find that we have nothing to share with others. We can certainly still be a help to others even when we don't have much for ourselves but by stretching ourselves beyond comfort and pushing toward creating a life of our own design, we'll then have the resources to share with others. Let me be clear, if you currently aren't in a position to help others with resources, I do not mean that you have settled for a mediocre life, I simply mean that by shifting our minds from only thinking of our own survival and stability can give us more motivation to think bigger.

Second, a life of mediocrity puts your own personal comfort ahead of the wellbeing of others. Yes, we are all responsible for taking care of ourselves but we are also responsible for supporting others during difficult times. If all I'm thinking about is my own comfort, then I will probably not be willing to part with anything that adds to my comfort and convenience such as money and material possessions. This thinking promotes selfishness and puts no demand on my talents to stretch beyond comfort and see what I am truly capable of. Statements like "It's not my problem" can become the mantra of someone who is only concerned with sustaining himself. YES, you should take care of yourself and YES, you should take care of your family. However, Lion leaders are always willing to set BIGGER goals that when accomplished can help them be able to support others in times of need. Warren Buffett is one of the wealthiest men in the United States and is known to be extremely generous. He has given away billions of dollars to various foundations that work to improve the conditions of people living around the world. By being a person unwilling to settle for mediocrity, he is able to help others in a bigger way. And, even if we never become billionaires, we can still stretch ourselves to reach our fullest potential both personally and professionally. This will give us more resources to be able to help with when we choose to do so. Choosing to play small may feel good in the moment because it is so comfortable, but it will cost you results and it will cost the rest of the world as well.

The challenge with change

Hopefully you're even more convinced now that it's time for you to step into your greatness than ever before. Let's talk about the transition that you'll experience as you transform from a person who may have settled for mediocrity in the past, into a LION leader who is boldly and courageously living to serve our world.

Russian philosopher, Isaac Asimov said, "Life is pleasant, death is peaceful. It's the transition that is troublesome." Transition is what many consider "no-man's land." It's the place where we move away from something that we've been holding onto for some time and venture out into the unknown. Whether you're transitioning from a relationship, a career, financial setbacks or simply an old mindset that has played a significant role in your past, transitions can be downright scary. We've seen that many people in an abusive relationship will stay in that relationship simply because they are afraid to make the transition.

People will also stay in a dead-end career, fighting feelings of fatigue, burnout and insignificance only because they're unwilling to endure the challenges that come during the transition to something better. It's no secret that our brains are hard-wired to seek pleasure, and one of our favorite pleasures is having certainty. We create "false" certainty in many situations just so that we can feel that we are in control. This is one of the main reasons why transitions can appear to be so difficult, it's because we feel like we are out of control. Well, let me let you in on a secret, control is an illusion. So is stability. If you have ever lost someone in a tragic accident or because of a health issue, you know that we really can't control anything. The only thing we can control is our response. Victor Frankl said in his best selling book, *Man's Search for Meaning,* "Everything can be taken from a man but one thing: the last of the human freedoms-to choose one's attitude in any given set of circumstances, to choose one's own way."

If we're going to get to the next level in our relationships, in our finances and in our physical health, we must get better at controlling the only thing that we can control, our mind. Here are a few things to keep remember as you prepare to leave old things behind and step into something new.

To produce differently, you have to think differently

Surround yourself with sounds, images and people that can keep you excited and believing for more. We are going to discuss the power of your thoughts in much more detail later in the book, but for now, just know that your thinking plays a critical role in your ability to stay the course amid adversity. If you are focused on what could go wrong instead of all the things that could go right, you will probably remain in a place of fear, unwilling to take the necessary steps to move forward.

Appearances don't matter

When we're in the midst of a change, the energy that we exert as we try to uphold an image of "having it all together" can prevent us from taking the necessary steps to move forward. Instead of trying to uphold an image, we should focus our energies on the process of creating as we remain humble and willing to make mistakes. Remember, failure is not the opposite of success failure is simply a part of success. Let go of prideful ideas that you must appear to be perfect and uphold an image. Forget the image and simply be willing to get to work.

Everyone can't go on this journey with you

The journey of success is one that we must be willing to walk alone. This is not to say that there isn't a need for support as we weather tough times. We will talk about support and teamwork later in the book. But for now, it is important for you to know that we can't wait until we have all the comforts of a personal cheerleading squad before we are willing to step out toward our goals. Elon Musk, CEO of Tesla and Space-X said, "Being an entrepreneur is like chewing broken glass and staring off into the abyss." There are times when we simply must do what we don't want to do even if that means standing alone. I have always believed that crowds don't typically travel very far anyway. Be okay with walking alone at times, the right people will show up when you when it's necessary.

You need to weigh the costs

For every choice we make there is a cost as well as a benefit. Yes, there are benefits to avoiding change, like immediate comfort but there are HUGE costs as well.

When we try and avoid the transitions that come when we move forward so that we remain comfortable, we actually avoid the work that is necessary for us to improve and move into the next level. By avoiding "the work" we lose self-confidence, motivation, accomplishment, and influence. These are essential elements of Lion level leadership.

When it comes to doing the often very challenging work, I am reminded of the quote that says, "If we do what is hard, life gets easier. If we do what is easy, life gets hard."

Challenge and difficulty are going to be part of your journey but if you truly want to grow into a stronger person, you must endure them. There can be no growth without transition. I have heard it said, "Growth is simply a continual interactive process." So, we must be willing to interact with our life by way of our choices and make the adjustments necessary as we move toward our desired destination.

It's also important to note that if we don't get a clear picture of what our final destination is, there will be too many opportunities to forget what we're working for, quit, and then retreat back to a life of mediocrity and comfort. Pushing through the transitions of change can be tough enough as it is, even with a clear picture of our desired outcome. But, without it, dealing with the challenges, fear, and frustrations that will definitely come may be too much to bear. Speaking of that, I want to share some tips that will help you once you begin the process of transition, or what I call, the "messy middle."

Transition Tip #1: Be intentional and create balance

Often we can be in such a hurry to rush through the process of a transition, trying to arrive at our destination, that we forget to keep other priorities in the right perspective. We can be so focused on achieving one goal that we lose sight of the reasons why we are working toward the goal in the first place. For example, a husband might tell his wife that she needs to understand his "disconnectedness and distance," as he is working hard to reach a financial goal. While there does need to be a mutual understanding, the pursuit of a goal is no excuse to punish the very people who we are working for, those who look to us for companionship, love and support.

Keeping the most important things important as we work toward the next level will always give us greater satisfaction in the end. A great friend of mine used to always say that we should never sacrifice our families on "the altar of success." As you're moving through a transition, don't forget to involve those closest to you and be sure to set clear parameters of non-negotiable family time to spend with those you love. Never forget that your attention is the rarest and purest form of generosity. So if you are thankful to have people on the journey with you as you move through your transition, don't forget to stop often and show them how much you care about them and that they have not been forgotten. You never want to be so focused on "getting to the top of the mountain" that you lose everyone else that was meant to be on the journey with you.

Transition Tip #2: Keep a record of the process

Sometimes we're so excited to just get through journey that we forget much of what the journey is about. When this happens, we can miss much of what we could have learned and experienced because we were rushing through the process. If we are thinking of ourselves as a teachers and mentors, we want to be able to pass on as much valuable information as we can to others while they are on their journey. So, don't forget to record some of what you think and feel as you walk through the good and bad times. It will be good for others to read about later, and therapeutic for you at the time that you're writing it. Keeping a journal is a great way to clear your mind and eventually pass on some wisdom.

Transition Tip #3: Take the transition one day at a time

All too often we become impatient during transitions and we miss new opportunities that be could headed our way because we're so focused on what we believe is not happening fast enough. Also, looking so hard at what we don't have yet can cause us to miss opportunities to be strategically resourceful with what we already have. Remember, pain is inevitable but suffering is optional. Don't make the transition more uncomfortable than it has to be by rushing the process and focusing only on what you don't have yet.

Transition Tip #4: Guard your mouth

As you work through transitions, and there will be many of them, it's important to avoid putting a lot of negative energy into the atmosphere with negative talk. Many times we simply aren't aware of what we're thinking and saying, but our words do matter even if what we are saying is unconscious. What we say, we hear! The more you allow yourself to speak negatively during a transition, the more damage that can be done and the longer it will feel like the transition is taking. The pressure that comes during transitions can provoke subconscious programs to be activated so try to be aware of what is coming out of your mouth because you do hear every word you say. Transitions are a time when self-awareness of how you're thinking and speaking is vitally important.

Transition Tip #5: Celebrate the small victories

I love celebrating the achievement of even a small goal. Whether it's buying myself a gift or taking the family on a trip, celebrating the small achievements can make the longest journey too short. Never forget that it's the small things that make life rich. Don't forget to shine the small trophies in your cabinet because they signify the battles won along the journey. Celebrating small victories can re-energize you and remind you that you are a WINNER. Remember that losers always focus on winners and winners always focus on winning. LION leaders are winners!

CHAPTER 2
What You Believe

"99% of the decisions that you think you are making in life, you're not making. Your belief systems are making them for you."

Brian Klemmer

Russian philosopher Isaac Asimov said, "Education isn't something that you can finish." While technical knowledge and practical skills are certainly a part of any ongoing education, I think it's even more important that we be willing to educate ourselves through daily introspection and the identification of our subconscious belief systems. As we do this, I believe that our capacity for wisdom and influence expands substantially.

Our challenge is that we often know what we know so well that we have a hard time seeing anything new. So here's a powerful question that I often ask: What story are you so afraid of letting go of that you can't embrace a new one? Maybe your story is that you've messed up too much or that you don't have enough education. Maybe your story is that you had one big opportunity for success earlier in your life but because it didn't turn out the way that you'd hoped, you'll never have another great opportunity again. Maybe your story is that you're too old, too young, too short, too fat, too different or just too misunderstood. Maybe your story is that you're too dumb, or just that you're too tired.

Maybe you believe that if you were just a little smarter, a little more attractive or had just a little more time and money that you'd finally have what it takes to go after your dreams.

All of these beliefs are lies **OR** they can be your truth. You get to decide!

The good news **AND** the bad news is that you will make yourself right! Whether you believe the best or the worst about yourself, those beliefs will always manifest in some way within the circumstances that you will create. You may not fully understand how much you care about "being right," but I can guarantee you that, on a day-to-day basis, you search for and gather evidence to prove just how right you are even if it means overlooking all the things that could prove something different to you. Psychologists call it "CONFIRMATION BIAS." This is where we look for and choose to notice only the things that reinforce our current beliefs.

It wasn't until I started facilitating leadership seminars around the world, with people from so many different backgrounds and with so many different belief systems, working to help them shift their mindsets, that I could have imagined just how important "being right" is to human beings.

The Power of Belief Systems

Albert Camus said, An intellectual is simply someone whose mind watches itself." In our world, where "busyness" seems to be a habit for so many people, I believe if we're not very careful we can allow old mindsets, along with marketing, advertising and the voices of the mass media to inadvertently determine the direction of our lives. Our direction leads to our destinations and our destinations lead to our destiny.

Years ago, my mentor said to me, "Ronnie, about 99 percent of the decisions that you think you're making in your life, you're not actually making. There's something that makes those decisions for you."

At first I didn't quite understand how something other than my own conscious thinking could direct so many of the decisions. My mentor went on to tell me that it was my *sub-conscious belief systems* that were the source of what I believed most of my options were. It was unknowingly from those very options that I was making my decisions. It wasn't the choices themselves that were the root of the problems, the root problem were the options that I believed I had to make my choices from.

You see, the options that you and I believe we have, as well as the possibilities we see for our entire world, are based upon sub-conscious belief systems. I've heard psychologists say that when we're born, we're born with only two fears— the fear of loud noises and the fear of falling. Ultimately, all of our other fears are learned. Other fears, which could include, meeting new people, starting a business, making a strategic investment or something like writing a book may be hold us back from living life to our fullest potential.

Our belief systems (including both rational and irrational fears) lead to the development of lenses through which we see ourselves and the rest of the world around us.

Imagine as I'm writing this that I'm wearing a huge pair of blue-lensed glasses. And, let's imagine that these lenses represent the belief systems or perspectives that I consciously and un-consciously have on the world. Let's also consider that I am wearing these BIG, BLUE lenses but have ABSOLUTELY NO IDEA THAT THEY ARE THERE! So again, I am wearing these goofy, blue glasses but I am absolutely oblivious to it. So imagine that every single time I look at something, I believe it has a blue tint to it. And over time, that blue tint becomes a perspective that is an "unconscious provoker" to many of my decisions. If I look at a blank WHITE canvas, which could represent all the possibilities of my future, I see a BLUE canvas! And if someone comes along and says, "Ronnie, what do you think of that white canvas?," I'm probably going to think to myself, "this person is out of their mind." Why?! Because it's OBVIOUS to me that the canvas is BLUE.

When two people on the same team or within a family see things differently based on their respective belief systems, their typical response is to shut down, pull back, stop talking, stop collaborating, and give up on the possibilities that are present. This is where many teams and families begin to fall apart. Not suddenly, but gradually! I often say that failure often occurs gradually, gradually, gradually, and then SUDDENLY. I don't believe that team members will INTENTION

ALLY shove each other off-course, but through differences of unaddressed perspectives (Belief Systems) the members of the team slowly nudge one another off the course through frustration, fussing and fighting. All of this, in hopes of defending lenses that they don't even know are there. _And again, they don't even know why they have the perspectives that they do!_ Understanding the power of these lenses, how they hold us back, and how we can use our awareness of them to better work together, is the key to TRUE, healthy progress.

It's important for us to remember that these lenses are just lenses. They don't represent who we really are, nor are they permanent. So instead of fighting to defend old belief systems that do not serve us, we must be willing to address and change them. It's pretty simple, but it's not always easy. You see, we tend to believe that our lenses _do_ represent who we are, and we unconsciously believe that our lenses are what is REAL. That's because unless we identify and address our lenses, they are all we've ever known. So our ego tells us that if we identify and attempt to change them, then we are changing the very thing that has helped us to survive. And, since survival is always our number one conscious and unconscious priority, the thought of changing can literally scare us to death.

We all have thousands of sets of lenses that pertain to every area of our life. We have lenses regarding how transparent we should be with other people. We have lenses regarding the types of conversations that we should or shouldn't have. We have lenses regarding what we believe our purpose in life is. We have lenses about personal responsibility. We have lenses about politics, religion, economics, the universe, commitment, trust and worthiness. We have lenses around how to handle resentment, how to get respect, and lenses regarding how to get love. All of these things drive the decisions that we make on a day-to-day basis and WE TYPICALLY DON'T EVEN KNOW WHERE THEY CAME FROM!

The Building of Beliefs

One of the most pervasive contributors to the development of our lenses is our perception of our past. When we experience hurts and pains, we tend to pack them up and carry them with us in the form of bitterness, regret and un-forgiveness. As a result, we unconsciously allow them to impact our present day life. Somewhere in our subconscious mind, we begin to believe that carrying these resentments will somehow keep us from being hurt again on a deeper level. It's not until we address the actual costs we're paying for this that we will become willing to change. The following equation shows how our lenses are created, and how, over time, they're reinforced again and again.

Circumstances + Details + Thinking + Feelings + Experience = Belief Systems

Every single circumstance we encounter has the ability to create new sets of belief systems. Our current belief systems determine so much of what we NOTICE in our present reality. (As well as the reality we will create in the future) Ultimately, what we notice in our current circumstances will reinforce our old belief systems. And, in addition to contributing to the actions we personally take and thus the circumstances we create, those old, reinforced belief systems become the standard for *how we label and pass judgment on ourselves as well as other people.*

Unless we address and step out of the vicious cycle caused by our own unconscious perceptions, we will live a life trapped in a matrix of judgments and labels. In other words, the reality we create on the outside will always be filtered through a subconscious set of belief systems that we have developed on the inside.

If I believe that what is coming *to* me is essentially coming *from* me, and that I attract and perceive certain things based on my own beliefs, I will be much more motivated to address what is going on within me. For example, if I believe that I am not smart, I will naturally avoid opportunities that could pull wisdom and insight from me and help me to grow. Likewise, if I believe that I'm not worthy of great success, I will only do things that pay me with AVERAGE rewards, or I will SABOTAGE the very things that bring the possibility of abundant rewards.

It all has to do with how right I need to be about my perspectives. James Allen, author of *As a Man Thinketh*, said, "The outer conditions of a man's life will always be found to be harmoniously related to his inner state. Men do not attract what they want, but that which they are."

Over the decade I've had the privilege of speaking to audiences in seven different countries. I have worked with thousands of individuals to help them uncover many of their limiting beliefs. The willingness to dive into the proverbial cave that we fear the most is often the key to creating large amounts of change in life.

Our internal dialogue often tells us to run from pain and unfamiliarity, and only run toward pleasure. However, when it comes to building strong relationships, successful teams and powerful families, facing fears and pushing through the pain are essential parts of the process. But, many people will only choose the easy road. I truly believe that nothing that is easy will ever make us proud. —Including addressing our limiting belief systems.

If we are not careful, our comfort becomes like an addiction. Too many times when we stretch outside our comfort zone, our self-preservation mechanisms kick in and begin to scream at us, "Pull back and get to safety because something is going on wrong!" In reality though, the pain of being uncomfortable COULD mean that we're actually on the right track and that we are approaching a threshold.

I heard a quote by Mahatma Gandhi many years ago that stated, "Man is at the center of a circle with no circumference." I believe this means that we live within a circle that has no limits. However, I do believe that in life, we often bump into our own self-constructed limitations on a daily basis.

And once we start to get close to these self-constructed limitations, feelings of worry, fear and uncertainty often cause us to pull back and stop stretching for the next level. These self-constructed limitations become constraints to our imagination in our own personal universe, which I call "mindset." And, we typically don't ever go to a place physically that we haven't first allowed ourselves to go in our imagination. To lead yourself like a LION, you're going to have to start thinking beyond the old "truths" that you once believed about yourself.

False Truths

Before I became aware of these subconscious belief systems, I believed that how I saw the world was reality. As a result, I was a victim to my limited perceptions. Those limiting perceptions were all around me. As a result, I would believe things like:

- I never want to try something new and fail, because I might look like a "failure."

- Confrontation is a bad thing and should always be avoided.

- I am entitled to a successful life even if I'm not disciplined.

- My family wasn't wealthy, so I can never be wealthy.

I could go on and on but I think you get the picture. It wasn't until I discovered these lenses and how much of an impact they were having on my life that I could do something about them. Awareness is the beginning of change! My limiting perspectives were keeping me from being bold, courageous and stepping into my role as a LION leader in the world.

The challenge with attempting to address limiting beliefs is that they're not always obvious. The first thing we must do is decide to play "detective." By playing detective you begin to look at your BEHAVIOR on a moment-to-moment basis. For example, showing up late to meetings is behavior. Not returning phone calls is behavior. Being rude, losing your temper and stopping communication are all behaviors. Engaging in gossip, always making jokes, being lazy, micromanaging teams and avoiding others are also examples of behavior.

Once you've identified a specific behavior, you must then reverse engineer the behavior and ask yourself, "What are the thoughts and feelings that I am having that are driving this specific behavior?" This detective work is a personal inward journey of introspection. This journey requires that you be willing to confront old ways of thinking and then make the proper changes.

For example, imagine that I was speaking to the participants of a leadership event. And, lets say that out of the audience of 100 people, 34 people raised their hand when I asked a question. When someone raises their hand, that is considered a behavior. The interesting part though is that we never really know what drives this behavior. This is why we each of us must do our own inward searching to find the thinking and the feelings that drive our behaviors. Some participants may raise their hand because their "lenses" tell them that raising their hand makes them appear intelligent. For some, raising a hand means they are a leader. Some may raise a hand as to appear interested in the content. Simply looking at behavior alone is not enough for us to uncover the underlying lens.

If we do not address the internal thinking and feelings that drive the behavior, our behaviors may never change. As a result, our behaviors will typically remain the same thus producing the same results. Change starts within and it requires confronting our internal thoughts. I believe we become "awake" when we are willing to confront our internal dialogue and make the adjustments necessary to behave differently. Everything else is simply living by default! Leaders are always on a journey of looking inwardly and seeing how they can become more valuable to the marketplace as well as the rest of the world. This means continually adding wisdom to our minds so that we can change some of our old perspectives and serve the world better. We can't wait for someone else to come along and get us motivated! We must be willing to look inwardly and "dig deeper" than what is comfortable and convenient to uncover some of these treasures of "awareness" that lie within.

Shattering Lenses

You must not be too hard on yourself for what you uncover when you're playing detective! As you start to ask yourself about the thoughts and feelings that are driving your behaviors, you should NEVER beat yourself up for what you discover. For this reason, many people choose to stay busy in life, jumping from one thing to the next and never taking time for the necessary self-reflection. They'd rather stay numb and unaware of the underlying issues that are so essential to change. Loving yourself throughout the process of transformation is VERY important. We must be willing to see the lenses for what they are, just lenses. These lenses of perception can be changed with practice. Some lenses are easy to change, and others are more difficult. So, we must be willing to wrestle with them if we are ever finally going to lay them to rest. By being willing to do the work, your eyes can be opened to a new world of wonder and awe. If we refuse to do the work, our life may be filled with boredom and burnout. Each moment holds within it the possibility of positive change. Harvard psychologist and author Ram Das says, "Each moment is rich with opportunity to experience the joys and pains of life. Each moment has within it a birth and a death, a loss and a gain. The true beauty of life is felt when we begin to open ourselves up past our own preconceived notions and experience the richness of each moment. This is living."

CHAPTER 3
Check Your Perspectives

"The secret of change is to focus all of your energy not on fighting the old, but building the new."

Socrates

On May 5th, 1961, astronaut Alan Shepard blasted off from near Florida's Kennedy Space Center to become the first American in space. The space race was already in full swing at the time, and the Soviet Union raised the stakes by launching cosmonaut Yuri Gagarin into space, making him the first person to orbit the earth.

This was a major disappointment to NASA, as they had hoped they would get Shepard to outer space first. But despite this seeming defeat, Shepard's mission still made a significant impact worldwide as it was watched by millions of people, thus cementing Shepard's legacy as one of this country's most beloved heroes.

As a result, Shepard was selected to be part of the first

Gemini missions later in his career. The Gemini missions were flown to help NASA get ready for the moon landings. Unfortunately Shepard's dream of being a part of NASA's greatest advancement in space exploration faced a significant setback when he was diagnosed with Meniere's syndrome.

Meniere's syndrome is caused by a fluid buildup in the inner ear, and it affects motion detectors within the brain. As a result, Shepard was forbidden from solo flights in jet planes or traveling into outer space.

Can you imagine the disappointment of spending your life hoping and preparing for something like this, only to have it taken away suddenly? If Shepard was anything like most other people, I'm sure he thought about the thousands and thousands of hours of mental and physical preparation he had invested in becoming an astronaut—and how it seemed like it was all for nothing.

But unlike how many people respond to setbacks, Shepard ignored any early feelings of frustration and discouragement and refused to give up. He simply decided to make some adjustments to his career and was willing to take over as chief of the astronaut office for NASA. In his new position, Shepard oversaw the activities of astronaut training as it pertained to mission planning.

In a few years, because of his commitment to the program, he was able to have surgery to correct the Meniere's syndrome and gain back his full flight status. Then, in February of 1971, Shepard landed on the moon. He celebrated the visit by unfolding a collapsible golf club and hitting two golf balls from the moon's surface. One ball is said to have landed in a crater. The other ball, Shepard said, went for miles and miles.

****

Understanding the purpose of events that have occurred in our lives is very important if we want to move forward with clarity, purpose, and power. What we are unwilling to address from our past will eventually catch up to us and confront us in our future. Unaddressed mindsets, paradigms, and programs, create a reality that we ultimately wind up living in.

Too many times we negatively label a challenging event and suppress the meanings instead of creating meanings that will motivate us to positively move forward with hope and optimism.

I once heard someone say, "Choosing to be positive in a negative situation is not called naive, it's called leadership."

Thus, your willingness to take control of your perspectives will undoubtedly influence your ability to positively lead others as well as yourself.

I constantly tell people that we are either winning or learning. There is no losing. And, when we are willing to look back on our past mistakes, past disappointments and unexpected outcomes, we can find lessons that will serve us as we move forward into the next level. By attaching a proper perspective, you can increase your capacity for more growth as a bold and confident leader. From this mindset we are able to create a future that is by design NOT by default.

Looking back at my life, I now understand that there are learning lessons in ALL things, and that we can learn valuable lessons simply by watching human behavior. Life on this earth is filled with opportunities for growth and maturity, and as we learn to strategically look back on our life's lessons, we can develop an enlarged and refined perspective on what is possible for our future. Being an architect for our future requires that we use the tools that have been provided to us. The ability to choose our perspective, during any circumstance, is definitely one of those tools. We must not forget it's power to serve us!

Would you say that your perspective on the events

from your past cause you to feel as happy and empowered? If not, the next question I have for you is, "Why not?" If I were to ask you about the events from your childhood that you believe made an impact on you, would you recall them in a way that causes you to feel powerful or would you say that these thoughts cause you to feel disempowered?

What you think about from your past, even as recent as yesterday, either causes you to feel positive and excited or negative and defeated. By being intentional with our perspectives, we start to create stronger, more positive feelings that give us much needed motivation to take positive action.

Alan Shepard faced many disappointments in his career, beginning with his belief that that he was going to be the first person into outer space, only to be surpassed by Yuri Gagarin just a few weeks before his planned mission. It is here though that I believe we get to see a great example of persistence and tenacity. It is often in the disappointing times that we make decisions that either lead to our desired destinations or to our defeat. Alan Shepard, and NASA, made the decision to continue on with their pursuits of being leaders in space exploration despite many initial disappointments and setbacks.

Just a few years later, Shepard would be grounded from space flight altogether when he developed Meniere's syndrome. Yet again, like a true leader, he persevered. If he would have allowed himself to take the perspective of a victim, he might have let feelings of resentment, disappointment and frustration to cause him to quit his pursuits of space, altogether.

Neil Armstrong once said, "Pilots take no special joy in walking, pilots love flying." If Shepard had allowed disappointment to cause him to pull back, stop believing and stop working hard, he could have settled into a life of mediocrity. But instead, he put his shoulder to the wheel, stayed in the work and eventually became the first man to hit golf balls from the surface of the moon. Shepard checked his perspective and as a result, made history.

Same Event, Different Meaning

One of the first leadership concepts that I was ever taught was that "THE FACTS DON'T MATTER!"

Now, as you read that, you may disagree and think, "Of course the facts matter. Results are everything!" Well, technically you're right. Facts and results are a great indicators of our progress. But, when it comes to keeping the right perspective and managing how we allow those perspectives to impact our state of being, those same facts and results have no more power than we choose to give them.

Let me explain.

When you and I "experience" any event in life, the event has no particular meaning until we assign one to it. For example, traffic was really congested this morning as millions of Americans drove to work. For some people, the meaning they attach to the traffic is, "This city stinks; they need more infrastructure. Politicians are idiots, and we live in a backwards country!"

However, some people will get in their car, sit in the same traffic, and while on their way to work, listen to an audiobook or podcast that adds value to their life. As a result, they appreciate each moment they get to spend in their car, even when they're in bumper-to-bumper traffic. They make the choice to see it as time well spent on an education. I call it "Windshield University."

Some people wake up, see rain outside and decide that it is going to be a "bad day." As a result, they go throughout their day looking for reasons to be right about how the day is bad. Some people decide that it's going to be a bad day even when they see the sun come up, simply because they've already decided that their life stinks. On the other hand, there are people who wake up, choose to be grateful for the day regardless of the weather, and make the best of every circumstance they encounter. Same day, *different meanings*.

To take it a step further, I've done trainings in which I've asked participants to share an event from their past and how they allowed that event to change their life. I'll never forget when a lady told me she had been through a divorce. When I asked her what she'd made the divorce mean, she replied, "It meant I was unlovable, that I did something wrong, that my parents were right about my lack of commitment AND that I didn't deserve love."

I then asked if anyone else in the room had ever experienced a divorce, and of course other hands went up. I turned to a lady who was sitting on the opposite side of the room from the first woman, and I asked what her divorce had meant to her. She had a completely different response. She had replied, "It meant I was free."

The second woman's response in comparison to the first one's, was eye-opening to the group. Both ladies had gone through a divorce but they had both made their divorce mean something completely different.

When I asked the other participants which one of the ladies was right, everyone agreed that they BOTH were. The reason they were both right is because they're the ones responsible for creating the meanings in their life. In the same way, you and I are also responsible for creating our own meanings. Yes there are tragedies in life, yes we are going to deal with many painful things, but how we decide to label those events with meaning will determine the quality of life that we live.

You and I are designing our future on a moment-to-moment basis with the decisions that we make. In every moment there's an opportunity to choose how we will respond to the circumstance that has already been created. We don't have to let disappointments cloud our vision for the future!

We can choose to look back at our life with what has once been seen as a disappointment, and use it as a lesson and opportunity for growth. Yes it takes work, but what's wrong with work? If you were going to build a house to live in for the rest of your life, I know that you would be very detailed about it.

So, why wouldn't you make the same effort when designing your future and creating your MEANINGS?

I would rather work at being happy than choose to be lazy with my mindsets, telling myself that I am always a victim and as a result, continuing to suffer. I have a friend who says, "If you'll be able to look back on this and laugh, why not choose to laugh at it now?"

Of course there's a time to laugh and a time to cry, but the point is, it's important to keep a positive perspective as much as we possibly can. You will have to carry the perspectives that you choose for much of the rest of your life, so why not choose to make them positive ones? Even though creating a "victim mindset" is a great way to get attention, sympathy, and control people through manipulation, it can rob you of your joy, self-confidence and self-image. Before we move on, please understand that I am NOT saying that there are never VICTIMS in life! But, there is a difference between being victimized and adopting a "victim' mindset. I personally have very close friends that have been victims of horrible accidents where they lost loved ones. What I am saying, is that we move through life, we must try our best to not allow an event from our past to keep us stuck in pain for the rest of our life. My friends walked through those horrible events and have since used those experiences to help others in need. They are true leaders and have inspired me to get rid of my excuses as I deal with much smaller challenges than the ones they have had to deal with. I am a better person for knowing them and having them speak into my life.

People either feel better after spending time with us or they feel worse! Rarely do we engage in a conversation with someone and leave it feeling the exact same way that we felt going into it. Self-awareness in this area is huge, and if we want to make a more positive impact on others, we must get control of our perspectives.

When Disappointments Become Victories

On April 24, 1990, NASA launched the Hubble Telescope into orbit. The Hubble was named in honor of Edwin Hubble, an American astronomer who, among other things, determined that the universe extended beyond the borders of our own Milky Way. Yet it had been nearly 40 years since the astrophysicist Lyman Spitzer had first had the idea of launching a telescope beyond the Earth's atmosphere.

The Hubble telescope represented an exciting new era for NASA, but as with most great achievements, there were some problems. The 2,000-pound, 9-foot-wide mirror on the inside of Hubble had been polished incorrectly. Though the mirror was off by just one-50th the width of a human hair, all the images that Hubble sent back to Earth were blurry. The images were no better than telescopes that were here on Earth.

It had taken 10 years and over 10,000 people working, to create the telescope. And once it was deployed, it didn't work as planned. Many people believed the telescope was a lost cause, a money pit, and that it wouldn't be worth the efforts that would be required to fix the problem. Newsweek even put a picture of the Hubble on the cover of their magazine, calling it "The $1.5 billion blunder." However, three years later, persistence and commitment paid off. The space shuttle Endeavor carried a crew of seven astronauts to fix the Hubble telescope during a five-day mission.

In December of 1993, the first clear images were sent back to Earth from the repaired Hubble, and they were breathtaking. What was once considered a huge failure had been corrected, and it now, even still, provides us with some of the greatest images and understanding of the vastness of the universe that we've ever had. In 1995 Hubble captured the image of what is now called "Pillars of Creation," which is almost certainly the most famous astronomical image of the 20th century. This image displays parts of the Eagle Nebula, which shows stars in the first phases of their formation. Hubble currently orbits Earth approximately 15 times per day and will potentially be replaced in 2018 by the James T. Webb telescope. The Webb telescope will orbit the sun and give us images from galaxies 100 times further away than Hubble.

As is the case with Hubble, a disappointment or failure doesn't have to be final. With persistence and patience, disappointment can be turned into an opportunity for victory. We are now enjoying the benefits of the work that was done on Hubble. Even though Hubble was initially expected to be usable for about five years, it has now been sending back images of our universe for close to 20 years. Talk about a disappointment being turned into something positive! Looking back on the examples of both Alan Shepard and the Hubble Telescope, we can see that keeping the right perspective on events that may at first seem disappointing, can lead us to great victories. It's in the disappointments that we learn to value victory. I always say to participants in my trainings, "challenges are inevitable but suffering because of them, is optional."

When we truly accept that the facts have no meaning until we attach a meaning, we take back our power to design the experience we want to have at any given moment. In my personal life, I repeat the phrase "Fact, Meaning" to reconnect to this concept and stay emotionally and mentally grounded. When I may have previously let circumstances determine my experience, I use the simple phrase, "Fact, Meaning" to get my head back into a proper place and continue creating the reality that I hope to create. When someone doesn't return my phone call in a timely manner, or opportunities don't come as quickly as I would like them to, I say to myself, "Fact, Meaning." When someone cuts me off in traffic, I say "Fact, Meaning." I am fully aware of the FACT, but I avoid attaching a MEANING to that fact that will leave me discouraged and defeated. I use this tool continually to keep my inward conditions guarded from negative interpretations of my outward circumstances.

I think it's always important to ask myself, "Out of all the ways I can look at this situation, what is the benefit I'm getting from choosing to see it THIS way? How does this serve my peace of mind?" It's when I forget to place a DIVIDER between the FACT and the MEANING that I start to believe that they are the same. When I buy into the

ILLUSION that the FACT and the MEANING are the same, I essentially create a false sense of certainty that may give me an immediate feeling of "rightness," but on a deeper level causes me to feel victimized and out of control.

When we take control of our perspective, we can remain more joyful and more focused on solutions that will make us more effective for our family, team and community. Not only does proper perspective pulverize painful interpretation, it also helps us to avoid procrastination. Procrastination is simply the CREATIVE avoidance of something that we have assigned a NEGATIVE emotion to. For example, if I believe exercising MEANS I'll have to experience pain, then I am more likely to avoid exercising. On the contrary, if I believe exercising MEANS I will experience more energy, more confidence, more passion and more productivity, that MEANING will typically overpower the payoffs of procrastination.

In many of the trainings that I do, I ask participants to think back to a time when they may have failed. As they think back on these events, I can actually see their physiology begin to change. I then ask the participants to share with the rest of the group, some of the thoughts and feelings they had during those times.

The responses are always similar, they will say that they felt unworthy, insecure, hurt or angry.

Next, I ask each individual to recall the three most dominant feelings that they experienced during the event. Next, I ask them to write those three emotions down on the left side of their paper. Once they have written down the three emotions, I ask them to write down an anecdotal feeling for each of the emotions listed. For example, beside "unworthiness" I have them write "worthy." Beside "insecure," I ask them to write the word "confident." Beside "timidity" they may write the word "bold."

Finally, I ask the participants to write a statement that includes those anecdotal feelings in the order that sounds best to them. An example statement might read, "I am a bold, confident and worthy leader."

These anecdotal feelings make up what I call their ***"Personal Leader Statement."*** By repeating our Personal Leader Statement again and again, we begin to "rewire" our thinking back to what it was before we allowed "negative" perspectives to condition us.

When I'm getting ready to speak at an event in front of an audience, I sometimes get nervous. When I feel that nervousness start to rise up, I always begin to recite my personal leader statement: "I am a bold, confident and worthy leader." I repeat it again and again! By focusing my attention on what I am, I do not let the nervous energy cause me to start doubting myself or focus on thinking negatively. In each moment, I can only focus on one thing at a time!

So when I speak these things to myself, it keeps me focused on who I want to be and helps me to stay grounded as I deliver my message to the group.

I recommend that you try this exercise yourself! Something powerfully positive happens to us when we shift our perspective from a place of disappointment and despair into boldness and confidence. By choosing to look at our life with a proper perspective, we can have better clarity and certainty on how to move forward with power.

Lastly, it is important to remember that you are not what happened to you. Failure is never final unless you decide for it to be!

Gratitude for your life, your family, your health and your team, infuses you with enthusiasm and power. On the contrary, when we begin to wrestle with our past as if it were some horrible monster, we waste so much valuable energy that could be used for positive creativity. I know that as I personally look back at pivotal times in my life that I once saw as negative, I now see them as they were—a necessary event to get me moving forward in the right direction. And as a result, I'm grateful for even the times that were the most difficult.

Someone once posed the question, "What if you woke up tomorrow with only the things that you had given thanks for today?" And Abraham Lincoln said, "We can complain because the rose bush has thorns, or we can be grateful that the thorn bush has roses." So the next time you begin to feel down about your life, I challenge you to write down 10 things that you're grateful for. Then, if you want to take it a step further, write down 20, then 30 and even 40 things you're grateful for. I challenge you to make a list of as many things as you can and keep that list close to you at all times. If and when you start to feel a little down, uninspired or ungrateful, simply pull out the list and start reading it aloud.

There are three things that I always say to myself to remain in a spirit of gratitude. First, I remind myself that many people fought and died so that I would have the freedom to do what I want to do with my life. Second, there are lots of other people in the world who have overcome much more challenging issues than I've had to deal with. Third, if I'm not grateful for what I already have, what makes me think I deserve more?

We are only temporarily passing through on this journey of life and our days are numbered. If we really want to make an impact on our world, we should first start by being grateful for all the things that we already have. No matter what we've been through, if we are willing to look hard enough, there is some silver lining in the cloud and there are some valuable lessons to be found.

CHAPTER 4

Leave the Past in the Past

"It's not the mountains ahead that we have to climb that wear us out; it's simply the pebble in our shoe."

Muhammad Ali

The space shuttle Discovery is known as the queen of NASA's space shuttle orbiter fleet, logging the most hours in space of any other orbiter. But things didn't start off so well for Discovery. The space shuttle was scheduled to take its first flight, known as STS-41-D, in June of 1984, from Kennedy Space Center. The countdown reached as far as engine ignition when there was an automatic shutoff that cut off the half-million gallons of fuel that would be thrusting into the engines. Apparently, a computer had picked up a problem within an engine valve and shut down the launch.

I will be using the story of the space shuttle Discovery throughout this chapter to remind you that we all must start somewhere when it comes to our biggest dreams, and we must also understand that there may be complications that cause us delay on the journey. But, we must not stop moving forward.

Can you imagine the missed opportunities that would have occurred if the corrections were not made to the space shuttle Discovery's initial launch? And what about the thousands of hours in space that would not have been logged if NASA hadn't carried on with the mission? No individual or organization that has ever achieved greatness in any area has allowed a challenge or setback to cause them to scrap their mission, ever. So why should you? **If you're looking for permission to quit, you will find it.** If you're looking for reasons to carry on and achieve the greatness that you dream of, you will find that as well. The latter simply requires a little more diligence and effort on your part.

As you look back on some of the stories of victory in your life, go back a little earlier in the stories to when they first began? Can you see that every single success story that you have experienced had a first step of faith that was required in order for you to begin?

Take your marriage for example. Think back to early in the relationship to the first date you had with your spouse. Or, think of your job! You can recall the first day in your office, or even better yet, the day when you applied for the job hoping to be hired. Maybe it was completing your education at a university, and you can think back to the first days on campus, or the day that you received the letter informing you that you had been accepted into the school. If you're a parent, you can probably remember the day that you found out that you were going to have a child and how all the excitement, nervousness and expectation were rolling together as you were about to embark on the journey of a lifetime. No matter what your story may be, I wanted to remind you that everything begins with a decision. My hope for you, as you read this chapter, is that you will look back at your life and give yourself a pat on the back, knowing that you did not quit. Even though you may not yet be the person you want to be, or the person you will eventually become, you are not who you used to be. All the mistakes that you've made in your life were made with the limited information that you had at the time that you made them. None of us know what we do not know, but many of us put unrealistic expectations on ourselves thinking that we should be further along, that we should have known better, and essentially, that we should have screwed up less. But the truth of the matter is, mistakes are simply part of the journey. They're meant to teach us valuable lessons about what and where we can improve. Remember, it's not how we make mistakes, but how we correct them, that will define us.

And the good news is, the journey is still not over! I often think of what I would say to my present self if I were already 50 years older, sitting on the front porch of my home, reflecting on my life. I am sure that I would have a much softer approach in how I talk to myself, and I would surely laugh a little harder at some past mistakes that I thought were so devastating at the time. I call this perspective my "future-self perspective," and it embodies the four qualities that we should all consider when we look back on our past:

Understanding

I heard a beautiful quote that says: "People don't always need advice. Sometimes all they really need is a hand to hold, an ear to listen, and a heart that understands." If you could go back in time to be there with yourself as you made some of your past mistakes, how would you treat yourself? Would you be kind, compassionate, and understanding? Or would you be rigid and condescending? I'm sure that as you look back at your life, you would probably wish you had been kinder to yourself. Since that is probably the case, why not be kind to yourself now? It really is the only time that we have.

Forgiveness

Until you learn to forgive yourself of all that you've done "wrong," or even what you have failed to do, you can't walk fully into the possibilities of tomorrow. Isn't it a huge ego trip to think that you don't deserve forgiveness? I mean, who do you think you are, carrying bitterness toward the person you were back then? What makes you think that you have the right to beat yourself up, day-in and day-out, over a mistake that you've already made? You don't, and it really is selfish to live in un-forgiveness because you are robbing the world of the joy that you could be sharing with it.

Wisdom

One of the things that I've learned is that the more wisdom a person has, the less arrogant and aggressive he or she is. Wisdom shows us that the human condition is a challenging one, and that many of the impulsive decisions made both by ourselves and by others, are made out of a survival mindset. We should never apologize for past actions that we felt we needed to make in order to survive. Survival is an instinct so ingrained in us that we often behave in ways that we're not very proud of. As we add wisdom to our mind, I believe our capacity for kindness, compassion and empathy, expands.

Non-judgment

All judgment is wrapped up in a need, the need to be right about someone or something. Being willing to release the need to be right and extend support instead, is definitely a quality that I hope my future self will possess. Walt Whitman stated, "It's OK to be curious, just not judgmental."

Positive Reflections of the Past

Muhammad Ali said, "It's not the mountains ahead that we have to climb that wear us out; it's simply the pebble in our shoe." So let's make the decision today that, no matter what issue is hindering our forward progress and representing the pebble in our shoe, we're simply going to remove it. Maybe it's anger, un-forgiveness or judgment toward past events that represents the pebble. Maybe you're more committed to being right about how you did something wrong, than you are committed to producing something amazing for those who will follow you. Maybe you believe that your perspective is the only one that matters, and that no one other than you can see things in a "proper" way. Maybe you'll carry un-forgiveness toward others and yourself and continue to waste so much of your creative energy reacting to something that is long over. It is the true definition of insanity to keep doing the same thing again and again while expecting a different result.

To create positive change, we must break the pattern of allowing our past to have anything at all to do with how we treat ourselves in the future. Yes, learn the lesson. Yes, grow from the experience. Yes, expand your understanding. But never use some old story that you've made up about yourself to contaminate the beauty of the present moment and all that is possible for your future. By focusing on how things used to be and all that you haven't done right, you wont be able to focus on all the possibilities that lie ahead of you right now.

I'm almost sure that as you read this, your old thinking patterns may prevent you from believing that all things are truly possible for you. But my question is this: Why do you need to be right about that? Why do you need to eliminate yourself from the game that is being played right now in life? The space shuttle Discovery went to space 39 times after it's first launch was delayed on the launch pad. Now, that same space shuttle sits in the Smithsonian Museum for thousands of people to marvel at each year. The markings and small damage on the orbiter tell a story of the journey that the Discovery has been on. And, while NASA saw the chips and damage to the orbiter as things needing repair, the Smithsonian now saw them as the "storytellers" of an incredible journey.

Years ago I heard this quote: "Life is like a game of chess. When the game is over, the queen and the pawn go in the same box." You see, we all have a death date, and at the end of our lives, the only thing that will have mattered is how we lived and what we created that will live on. The space shuttle Discovery carried 251 astronauts into space and obviously made a huge impact on each of them. It deployed the Hubble Telescope in 1990, and as a result, our view of the universe has expanded beyond what we could have ever imagined.

The International Space Station was built, one piece

at a time, by what the space shuttle Discovery delivered to it from Earth over the course of thirteen separate journeys. Now, the International Space Station is the largest structure in orbit—about the size of a football field—and at an estimated cost of $150 billion, it's the most expensive manmade structure in existence. So without the Discovery doing its part, and the commitment of many engineers and scientists looking beyond the shuttle's early problems, international space relations as we now know them today, would not exist.

We all have a responsibility to stretch beyond what we already know AND what we've decided about our past. By doing so, we get committed to where we can go in the future. And if we do look back, it should simply remind us of the richness of our journey. Maya Angelou said, "I wouldn't take nothing for my journey." So whether we see our past as good or bad, there's always much to be learned. As a LION leader, I recommend you ask yourself a few questions when you take time to reflect.

Question #1: What are some of the positive qualities I have exemplified along my journey?

I call this process "Identifying the Champion Within." Too often it's easy for us to only look at the negative things that we've done and not focus on what we've done well. In fact, after being a part of so many leadership seminars over the years, I have seen firsthand how many people tend to overlook the good that they have brought to life. Too often, we focus so much on the pain that we have felt because of disappointments and letdowns that we can't seem to notice anything else. These negative feelings often stick with us much longer than the positive ones because we replay the stories in our mind again and again. By choosing to look at what we've done well, we create more of the emotions that I believe will support us with positive accomplishment. Replaying a time when we exemplified courage, bravery, passion or excitement, can recharge our batteries and remind us of all the amazing things that we are truly made of. I believe that as we choose to look back on life, identifying the good qualities that we have, we will see that all the good things that we have done, far outweigh the bad.

Question #2: What are some of the highlights that I can remember when I want to feel joy, inspiration and

motivation?

Our life is moving at such a fast pace that many of us overlook the very things that can bring us the most joy; and truthfully, even the smallest things, done well, can do just that. For us to pass on to the next generation, things of value, we must first identify what things are valuable to pass on. We know that material possessions lose their zeal after a while, and that money, without a proper understanding of it, can actually do harm. I always say that more is caught than taught. So, I want to make sure I am passing on joy and a passion for life that can only come by focusing on the good things.

Question #3: To whom do you owe a thank-you?

Think back on all the people who have impacted your journey along the way. Have you ever taken time to simply say "thank you." I believe that people come into our lives for a reason, a season, or a lifetime. I often think back to the life links that I have experienced and how one person led me to another, who led me to another, and now, as a result, I've moved into the next level of success. When we're kind to people along the way, we add the much-needed fuel of love and compassion to the equation, and as a result, we help others and ourselves to feel better. I truly believe that love is the only thing that when given away comes back in greater supply.

In my own life, the times that I have sent a simple note or made a phone call with the sole intention of saying "thank you" have led to some of the richest conversations I've ever had. Jim Rohn said, "What is easy to do is also easy not to do." Saying "thank you" is a simple thing to do, but we rarely take the time to actually stop all that we are doing to simply say it.

LION leaders make a habit of honoring the highest thoughts that tell them to be kinder than necessary and to take time to let others know how valuable they are. Our words are weapons that we can use to build up those around us, including ourselves, or tear them down, just the same. Why not use this as a reminder to make a list of a few people you could thank and then reach out to let them know? I believe that from a simple act of kindness, you can start to feel stronger regarding purpose and contribution in your life.

Question #4: Who do you need to forgive?

I often say that forgiveness is the key that unlocks the door to the next level. I don't choose to forgive people because I'm weak; I forgive them because I am strong enough to understand that people make mistakes. When we come from a place of forgiveness, we unload our backpack of the large stones that we placed there, when we focused on how others may have treated us wrong. Forgiveness is said to be the *final form of love*. In leadership trainings I always ask the audience, "Who here today has ever been hurt by someone?" Almost all the hands in the room go up! I then tell the group that if their hands are not up, they just need to just keep living because at some point they will experience hurt.

At Cape Canaveral, when the Challenger space shuttle exploded on January 28th, 1986, killing seven of the crew onboard, many fingers were pointing in many different directions placing blame. However, it was decided that the only way to move forward was to forgive the mistakes that had been made and to carry on more intelligently in the future. Many of the people within NASA felt much guilt regarding what should have been done differently to prevent the disaster. There was a two-and-a-half-year grounding of the space shuttle fleets until flights resumed with a mission flown by the Discovery space shuttle.

No matter what we've been through, the fastest known way to heal is through forgiveness, not blame or revenge. People who use revenge to settle the score only suppress the feelings of pain deeper and later mix them with new feelings of guilt.

This doesn't mean that forgiveness should put you in a position to be taken advantage of or hurt repeatedly. As President John F. Kennedy said, "Forgive your enemies but don't forget their names." Thankfully, the people at NASA were able to forgive one another of past mistakes and continue pursuing their goals of space exploration.

Guarding Against Past and Present Baggage

Can you imagine the response from my friends at NASA if I were to have said, "How can I help you to get to the moon?" I'm sure that anyone who heard this question would have thought, "Does this guy not know that we're now going to Mars?" It's important to remember that our past has gotten us to where we are, but in no way should the past act as a hindrance to keep us from where we're headed. Yes, the moon landings were incredible accomplishments, but were only a stepping-stone to our exploration of deeper space.

Novelist Margaret Drabble said, "When nothing is sure, everything is possible." One of my greatest frustrations in life is the number of people who seem to believe that they fully understand all that is out there in the universe.

My first on-site experience at Kennedy Space Center exposed me to many individuals who have worked for many years in the field of space exploration. And it was clear by listening to some of their experiences at NASA, that none of them believed they already had it all figured out. I decided that if some of the smartest people in the world were open-minded and passionate about learning new things, my level of open-mindedness could definitely improve. I have begun to question everything about what I think I know, and as a result I feel that I have a deeper understanding of who I am and the purpose that I will fulfill while I am alive. The passion and intensity of some of NASA's team members even stirred a passion within me to learn more about our universe. These people have spent years of their life researching and studying data to prove that we may not be right about what we think we already know.

I call this spirit of open-minded curiosity, "living in the question." When we live in the question, we begin to approach each day with the wisdom and lessons from our past while not using them to blind us from the possibilities of the future. Unfortunately, so much of what we hear and see today is noise created by all the dramas of war, politics and terrorism. We're so provoked to think only of surviving that we take very little time planning and preparing for the future that we hope for.

Case in point: Every four years in the US, elections occur, and each election is said to be the most important election of all time. In reality though, the past proves that no matter who is in office, not much changes. Jim Rohn used to have what he called his "not much" theory. When a Republican gets into office, what changes? Not much. When a Democrat gets into office, what changes? Not much.

Yet, as of this writing, our nation is still reeling from the election of Donald Trump in November of 2016. We have all been duped into playing this roller coaster ride of politics for so long, that we begin to feel guilty even if we choose not to "buy in." Both Donald Trump and Hillary Clinton supporters are angry and protesting, jumping on social media and cable news networks to spew their hateful opinions. But, how many of those same people who have allowed the election results to negatively impact their personal lives are actually taking the time to work on their passions, pursue their goals and develop the disciplines that will enable them to have a better future? Probably not too many.

As a LION leader, you must guard your passions and your energy. The way you do it is to guard your mind. If you allow politics, sports or religious debate to get you so fired up that you lose the energy that you could be utilizing to achieve your own goals and dreams, you've been duped.

Many people benefit from your weaknesses but you must learn to profit from your strengths. We shouldn't rely on the mass media to give us our facts. If you don't believe me, simply research the Gulf of Tonkin incident and how our American government as well as citizens responded to an incident that was simply false.

We must be careful of whom we trust, what we believe and how we allow those things to affect our emotions. You must guard your eyes, your ears and even your mouth, if you want to create a future by design. Media companies spend billions of dollars each year to figure out how to get and maintain your attention. If left unaware, these companies can sneak in and take control of your subconscious mind, and lead you as a sheep to the slaughter.

You and you alone are the master of your destiny. Don't allow the mass media, social media, or anyone else for that matter, to determine your future. To be a leader, you must learn to lead yourself.

CHAPTER 5

Adopt a LION Mindset

"I failed my way to success."

Thomas Edison

If we're ever going to create the results we say that we want, we must be willing to think in new ways, stop having to be right about old mindsets, and move into a more focused and intentional way of living.

In short, we have to adopt what I call a the "LION Mindset."

I'm going to share five concepts that we must keep in mind if we want to think like a LION leader.

1. Everyone is judging you

This may sound harsh but it is absolutely true. Because everyone is judging you and everyone else as well, any judgment on you loses much of its effect.

Fearing what other people think will give you permission to keep doing things the way that you've always done them. This fear falsely places other people in control of your life. When we fear what other people think, we inadvertently shift from a responsible mindset to a blaming mindset. As a result, we allow other people - who are, above all else, just trying to pay their own bills and keep a roof over their heads, to determine OUR future. Giving anyone, whether it's a family member, a friend, a co-worker, or a neighbor, power to negatively influence your decisions is simply foolish.

In a world full of so much noise, people are thinking about the thousands of images that they're bombarded with, day-in and day-out, along with the challenges that they're already facing. When it comes to basing your life and your decisions on the judgments of others, consider this phrase: Out of sight, out of mind. There's only so much mental capacity that a person has, and I can tell you that once you leave their presence, people are nowhere near as concerned with you as you think they are.

2. People only show you what they want you to see

A simple scroll through your social media feed can have a disastrous effect on your mindset as you start to compare your life to the seemingly "perfect" lives of others. But know this: You're comparing your private thoughts and fears to a carefully crafted image that people have designed for their "internet friends."

The problem with comparing your life to the "internet lives of others" is that it develops a "Keeping up with the Joneses" attitude. And, the Joneses are probably frustrated, insecure and simply trying to figure out how to make their own life work. People have addictions, extramarital affairs, abuse, neglect, fear, anxiety, worry, and a slew of other things that they do not want you to know.

In order to adopt a LION mindset, you'll have to stop comparing yourself to others, and you'll also have to stop trying to impress people with a false facade. You should aim to impact people through kindness and service, not by having better clothes, a bigger boat, a nicer car, or more social media followers. Remember, everyone has a chapter in their life book that they will never read out loud. Look at what you have with gratitude, not comparison. John Dryden said, "Jealousy is the jaundice of the soul."

3. Most people are opportunists

The loyalty of many people is found in opportunity, and that isn't necessarily a bad thing. I've noticed that some of my best relationships are with people who are pushing to better take care of themselves and their families. They don't want to start drama or pick fights with anyone! Instead, they are pushing to bring their hopes and dreams to pass.

In other words, some "selfishness" is okay, as long as it serves the overall purpose of contribution to our planet. Remember, if you get really aggressive with your goals and dreams, your passion and motivation will rub off on others. I often say, "Leaders should move so quickly toward their goals that they create a jet stream that pulls other people into their greatness."

Pursing your dreams with focus and intention is a great way to help others achieve their dreams as well.

4. There are no guarantees in life

If you really want to adopt a LION mindset and embrace all that life is about, do what Tim McGraw said in his hit song, and "Live Like You Were Dying."

Our submersion into a culture filled with constant

information and marketing keeps us stimulated and looking for the "next big thing." As a result, we often overlook the most important things that are in front of us. When you take the things that you've been given for granted, and only focus on what you want to have or achieve, you never fully experience all the richness and fulfillment that life has to offer.

There are no guarantees in life! The people, as well as the possession we've worked to hard to have, can be here today and gone tomorrow. Sometimes the best thing we can do is to stop trying to figure out where we are going and simply enjoy the place right where we already are. It's called being present and it un-attaches us from the illusion of "form."

5. You, and you alone, are responsible for your outcomes

If you want more, you must be willing to become more. Each new level of success you move into will require a new version of yourself. Please understand, becoming a newer, better version of you comes at a cost. My wife and I like to invest at-least an hour of our day into a physical health routine that helps us to get better everyday.

-Exercising each day costs me my old story

It may not seem like much, but when we've gotten comfortable with our story and with the reality that we have created with it, letting go of an old story can be tough. You see, when I was younger, I was a skinny kid. I never had lots of muscle. However, as I began to exercise my body regularly during college, I began to see my body change substantially. And with that, I had to leave the old story and image of myself—one that I had known all my life—behind.

One of the main things you and I must learn is to release our limiting stories about who we are and what we cannot do. Many of the stories we carry around as adults were created when we were children. Think about that for a second! We're all allowing a young, immature, sheltered, and naive version of ourselves to make many of the adult decisions that we face on a daily basis.

Whether you acknowledge it or not, your mind is so powerful that if you subconsciously continue to be right about the stories you've made up in the past, you will continue to look for ways to reinforce those beliefs and create more of what you already know. In other words, you must be careful what you say to yourself because it will determine the actions that you take and the results that you produce. New and better thinking leads to new and better actions. Better action leads to better results.

-Exercising costs me my time

An hour each day to exercise my body and clear my mind is a small investment considering the payoff that I receive from it. I can't think of any investment of my time that will pay me the dividends that I receive from strengthening my body. When I discipline my body, I am also strengthening my mind. Investing time each day into my own physical health reminds me that I AM WORTH IT and gives me better endurance as I push toward other goals in my life.

-Exercising costs me comfort

If you don't already have a regular workout routine, this one may be a big deal for you. However, if you want to find some motivation to get off your butt, just go to Walmart, walk around, and look at the fitness levels of those who are there.

Sadly, many people have been duped into believing that

buying the newest pill, outfit, or soft drink, will make them permanently feel better and mask the pain they experience because of being unhealthy.

Now that I have listed the costs of exercising each day, let's look at the benefits:

Exercising gives me clarity

My mind works many, many times better when I've gotten my blood pumping and sweated out many of the toxins that I've taken in the day before.

Exercising motivates me

When I challenge myself by pushing myself physically first thing in the morning, it stirs my motivation to accomplish more as the rest of the day goes on. As I see myself getting stronger, I am motivated to push myself in other areas of my life.

Exercising builds confidence

When your body starts to look healthier, you begin to develop a healthier self-image, and that translates to greater confidence. All physical growth begins with mental discipline. When we discipline our mind, our body will soon follow. Physical health is a mental thing.

Exercising increases my mobility

Getting older takes a toll on your body! Anyone who is up in their years will tell you that somewhere between the ages of 30 and 40, our metabolism starts to slow down and our joints begin to tighten. When this happens, it's harder to function doing day-to-day activities. When we stretch our muscles with a proper exercise routine, our body rewards us with better mobility and higher energy levels.

Exercising instills trust in myself

The more I push myself to get up and exercise each day, even when I may not feel like it, the more I trust myself to do other things that I know I need to do. When I can trust myself to do the work, even when it is uncomfortable, I begin to trust myself to follow through on other tasks that lead to success.

Exercising kick-starts momentum

Nothing will kick-start your day like getting your blood pumping and your heart racing through a strong exercise routine first thing in the morning. This momentum will undoubtedly carry over into other areas of your life throughout the rest of the day. I always say, "Start strong, finish strong." Exercising first thing in the morning sets the pace for a stronger, more productive day.

Exercising provides self-respect

Your own physical health is one thing that no one can ever take away from you. When you develop the disciplines that so many people overlook, you begin to see yourself as a warrior with self-respect. I also want to note that exercising is a privilege. Many people are born with, or develop, disabilities that make exercising difficult. If you're healthy and have the ability to get up each day and move your body, you should not take that for granted.

Healthy Body, Healthy Mind

So why have I spent so much time discussing physical health? The answer is this: How you do anything is how you do everything! Here's the hard truth: If you won't honor yourself, it probably won't take much for you to give up on another goal or a dream when resistance eventually comes. In fact, when I coach people on a personal level, I always require them to be a part of an exercise group or routine. Unfortunately, we're often too afraid of the accountability that comes when we make ourselves part of a group. We often choose to remain isolated, and that isolation breeds complacency. When we get a bigger picture of ourselves than the one offered to us by our dumb-phones and television sets, we can clearly see that how we conduct every area of our life really DOES MATTER. And, when we know that we have a job to do, and that the only way to complete that job is to operate at our fullest potential, certain behavior is no longer allowed. I've heard it said, "Success starts with a YES and is maintained with a lot of NO's. Start saying YES to your physical health goals and NO to any image of yourself that is not healthy. How you see yourself in your mind will happen in time.

Below are some of my LION mindset
"NONNEGOTIABLES."

Non-negotiable #1: Never abuse drugs or alcohol.

All we have to do is look at the abuse that has cost many people their families, their careers, and their health, to see that the path of drugs and alcohol leads only one way - to death and destruction. If you feel you may have an issue, get help immediately because this issue will not take care of itself. What we turn a "blind eye" to today becomes a "blind spot" tomorrow. There is no faster way to have and accident and wreck your life than to turn a "blind eye" to an addiction. Life does not improve naturally, life improves intentionally.

Non-negotiable #2: Don't spend time in toxic environments.

A toxic atmosphere can be one in which there is constant drama, fussing or fighting. But, in my opinion, a toxic atmosphere can also be one in which the people present are not doing anything significant with their lives. The attitudes and beliefs of others rub off on us very easily, and if we're going to make the most of this life, we must be very careful of whose energy we're willing to carry as our own. Remember, you become like the atmosphere that you are in. If you want to create better results, create a better atmosphere to spend your time in.

Non-negotiable #3: Don't associate with negative people.

My rule is this: If you can't see my greatness, then I don't care to see yours. It may sound selfish and self-centered, but you only have so much relational energy to spend, so spend it well. Don't associate with people who can't see your potential and refuse to push you to reach it. Misery loves company!

Non-negotiable #4: Avoid spending time with narcissistic people.

I don't spend time with people who only know how to talk about themselves, or who make every story swing back around to them. Spending time with someone who believes that his or her goals are better than those of others is not only a waste of time, but it is also extremely frustrating. Lion leaders are more concerned with being *interested* than they are being *interesting.*

Non-negotiable #5: Don't spend time with apathetic people.

People who don't care about *anything* typically don't care about *anyone.* If a person doesn't care about others, I don't spend much time investing in them.

Non-negotiable #6: Don't associate with rude people.

The moment that someone shows me who they truly are, I believe them. I don't need relationships enough to continue to associate with anyone who is rude to me or anyone else. I want to work with people that are passionate AND compassionate. None of us are perfect, but we can surely make the effort to be kind to others. To me, rudeness is a sign of insecurity, fear and doubt. I have found the most powerful influencers are the ones who are the kindest to other people.

***The LION MINSET also means....

I put my family FIRST...

I am so blessed to have an amazing family! My mother and father have always exemplified hard work, honesty, integrity and kindness. There is no way that I could have asked for better parents. My parents didn't grow up in the most perfect conditions though. As I was growing up, I witnessed distant family members that dealt with addictions, abuse and even incarceration. The pain that those experiences caused my immediate family was a catalyst for me to learn as much as possible about "self help" and "personal development." I'm very proud of all of my family! Though I've not been perfect by any means, I decided years ago to adopt a LION mindset to be the best I could be. I committed to be an encourager, and to always try to see the best in others. My decision to pursue personal development doesn't mean that I think I'm better than anyone else, it means I've simply committed to learn my craft well so that I might add value to those around me. Because of my family, I am who I am today.

As we begin to adopt the LION mindset, there are a few things that we may encounter along the way. The things are definitely worth mentioning below. Hopefully, being aware of these things will help you to deal with them in a healthier way.

People will be uncomfortable

Your willingness to stretch for more can often cause people to judge their own life, compare it to yours and as a result, feel uncomfortable. As you know, comparison is never a good thing because it can cause us to think more highly of ourselves than we ought to, or to think less of ourselves than we should. Either way, comparison is an inappropriate way of gauging our own life's journey. LION leaders must know, without a shadow of a doubt, that they have the strength to walk certain parts of their life alone, and that not everyone will be coming along the journey with them. Yes, our choices may make other people feel uncomfortable but we must remain true to ourselves.

People will assign false motives to you

No matter who you are and how positive you try to be, you will encounter someone along your journey that will try to disrupt your life with negative accusations. I have had a share of my own. However, when you're more committed to learning and leading than you are to being offended and upset, you will move much more quickly toward your desired outcome and enjoy the journey much more along the way.

You will fail at some point

NASA is known for saying that "Failure is not an option." But, I personally believe that failure should be an option and that we should actually learn to embrace it.

You see, when we fail, it simply means that we are trying something new. It means that we're stretching for something more, and that we have a goal that is bigger than what we've already achieved.

Never let anyone convince you that the best way to become successful is to avoid failure. Thomas Edison actually said, "I failed my way to success." Now consider all the attempts that he made to create something significant, and how many times he found an alternate approach after never giving up. Don't worry about all the people who may be judging you. As previously mentioned, if someone puts you down and chooses not to encourage you, he or she doesn't deserve a seat on your life-bus.

You will begin to doubt yourself

For many years, I would go to bed at night questioning whether or not I should just give up on my dream and find a more "normal" job. When the money was tight and there were bills past due, I questioned everything about myself. It was during those times that I found myself clinging to my faith, and to my wife, to find the much-needed support to get through another days.

I can remember when being asked to speak at an event for $300 was such a big deal that I would rack my brain being nervous and over-preparing. When we doubt ourselves, we tend to make things much harder than they need to be. You've probably heard it said that doubt has killed more dreams than enemies ever have. As a LION leader, when you begin to doubt yourself, you must quickly shift your thinking to more positive images, considering what could go well as you perform to the best of your abilities. It's those types of mental pictures that can pull us through the toughest times in our journey and give us the much needed inspiration to keep pressing toward the mark.

You will get angry

I can remember times in my life where I was willing to get so angry with myself for past mistakes, poor judgments, and bad decisions. All of these are an important part of the journey, though. Anger can be a fuel that, if used properly, can force us into taking some immediate action in a positive direction. However, carrying anger for too long can have terrible consequences. On this journey, be careful to guard and protect those around you while you are pushing through the challenges. The mistake that many people make is that they take out their frustrations on those they care most about. This not only leads to disappointment, but also heartache and pain for everyone involved. And, when we boil anger down to it's true essence, we find that it is primarily an ego trip that in some way gives us a subtle "payoff."

You will lose relationships

As hard as it is for me to admit, I have made many mistakes. Sometimes I've inadvertently taken people for granted; I've hurt the people I cared most about, and I've allowed good relationships to deteriorate into something unhealthy. In the process of pursuing your goals and dreams, try to keep a pulse on your relationships and take the necessary steps to keep them healthy before they become sick and toxic.

Keep in mind, we are all self-serving to a certain degree, so sometimes it's just best for relationships to end. I believe it is important for those relationships to end well, so that there is no negative residue with us when we move into the future. I've always said, how we finish one thing is how we start the next. So, if you need to end a relationship of any kind, do it with honor and compassion. You will be glad that you did.

Adopting a LION mindset is such a critical part of your leadership journey, so you need to be intentional about staying in a positive frame of mind as you choose to step out of your comfort zone and move toward your goals.

You were designed for such a time as this! No one on earth has the unique gifts and talents that you do, so use your uniqueness to find your unique path, and walk it with your own unique way.

And, don't forget to enjoy the process. So often, when I talk about LION leadership, many people think it means to jump into fight mode, ready to attack any obstacles that come their way. While staying on the offensive is very important as a LION leader, please understand that every step of the journey is what makes life rich, and each moment is full of opportunity. We must not get in such a rush to accomplish goals that we forget to actually live life along the way.

Along the way, remember there are many people rooting for you. I truly believe that it is the prayers of my parents and grandparents, along with those of myself, that have made all the difference in my world. Sometimes there will be unexplainable things along your journey that you will not understand, and I believe that much of it has to do with things that were done and spoken before our journey even began. Knowing that you have someone on your side, in your corner, who sees the best in you and wants the best for you, can help to lessen some of the negative emotions that can come when you step out on your own.

And lastly, I want to remind you that nothing incredible has ever been created from within a comfort zone. Just like working out, when you feel the pain in your muscles and you want to quit, that is the time when you're actually benefitting the most.

Whether mentally or physically, the most growth we will ever experience will come when we have broken away from our comfort zones and pushed through the limitations that can un-intentionally lead to mediocrity.

As the Mouth Speaks, the Mind Follows

I want to make a final note about LION mindsets. I talk repeatedly about guarding our mouth to ensure that we are not putting any negativity into the atmosphere that will derail us from our path. So instead of just avoiding saying the WRONG things about your future, I want you to be intentional about saying the RIGHT things. What can you tell yourself everyday that will shift your mindset into a more positive state and help you to focus on your path and where you're headed?

I have recently developed my own new bold declaration, and it reads:

"The experience I create in my life is my responsibility and no one else's. What I say I desire, I must be willing to create."

I am now challenging you to take some time to get absolutely clear about what you want to create, and the prices you're willing to pay to achieve it. Write it down, say it out loud ever day, and watch as your LION mindset begins to take more shape.

CHAPTER 6

Think Forward

"Our lust for comfort murders the passions of our soul."

Kahlil Gibran

Now that we've discussed how to shift our perspectives from things that have happened in the past, we need to address how we can better look toward the future. Many of the people that I have had the pleasure of working initially seem to be living a life of "probability" versus "possibility." Probability thinking considers what is expected based on things that have already occurred, while possibility thinking is more open and free of attachments to any old events and expectations.

In order to create something new within our team, family, or organization, we need to shift to more into more of this possibility thinking. Please note, probability thinking is extremely important! Thankfully, skilled doctors, engineers, scientists, pilots and astronauts all use probability thinking to make safe assessments that can literally save lives.

However, as we look forward to the future and pursuing our dreams, using the same thought process we've always used will inevitably lead us to more of the same results. It's when we truly think outside the box, or as some would say, think as if there is no box, that the world we've never even imagined begins to open up to us.

If someone would have told you 25 years ago that you would be able to use a phone to connect wirelessly with another person anywhere in the world, in real time, and be able to talk face-to-face using a camera that was built into that phone, you might have thought he or she was crazy. In other words, a lot has changed! We now see technology exploding onto the scene with new inventions that make inventions of even just a few months ago obsolete. And, how does that happen? People are thinking outside the box!

Here's an extreme case of out-of-the-box thinking: On November 26th, 2011, NASA launched the Curiosity Rover from Cape Canaveral, FL. The Rover then traveled through space on a journey of 350 million miles, after which it touched down on Mars just less than nine months later. The Rover's goal was to gather climate and geologic assessments while conducting potential planetary habitability studies in preparation for future human exploration.

So let's back up a bit: First, to think of sending a robot over a quarter of a billion miles away is pretty crazy on its own. Then, to have someone control that robot remotely, as it navigates new terrain to prepare for human exploration *of another planet*—to many, that wouldn't even seem like a possibility. But to those who think outside of the box, it is now reality. I heard a quote by a man named Lou Tice. He said, "Yesterday's dreams become tomorrow necessities."

As leaders, our job is to lead in such a way that we inspire others to give and **BE** their best. However, if we allow probability thinking to limit the potential effectiveness of members of our team, then we're not leading to the best of our abilities.

Too often our own scarcity thinking causes us to micromanage others and limit their productivity. As a result, we keep people on a short leash and we never fully empower them to be their best.

This can happen within our own families as well! People want to be led by inspiration NOT by control and manipulation. Leaders become great not because of their power over others but because they have learned to *empower* others. As we press toward the future, our forward movement should be so strong that our jet stream pulls other people into their greatness.

So how do we create this jet stream? We do this by learning to develop and practice possibility thinking. This type of thinking is critical and necessary as we develop into a more forward-thinking leader.

The following are five characteristics that every forward-thinking leader **MUST** have.

Passion

Many people die around the age of 30, but they're not buried until they're 80. In the meantime, they walk through life without passion and are virtually sleeping zombies. Their focus is not on what they could be doing; their focus is on where they've already been and what they've already done. As a result, a compelling future is no longer even possible in *their* minds.

But being busy and working hard doesn't necessarily imply passion. Passion is what it's called when we work hard for something we love. Stress is what it's called when we work hard for something we care nothing about. It has been said that the most powerful weapon on earth is the human soul on fire. Steve Jobs, founder of Apple, said, "The only way to do great work is to love what you do. If you haven't found it yet, keep looking," he says, "and never settle." Similarly, artist and poet Kahlil Gibran said, "Our lust for comfort murders the passions of our soul."

As I've said so many times before, comfort is the **ultimate addiction.** When we lead people, more will be caught than taught. Many people have insights that are valuable, but because they are not wrapped with passion, their insights fall on deaf ears. When our team can see that we're passionate about our work, we create an atmosphere in which others will be passionate as well. Great leaders don't tell you what to do; they show you how it's done—with passion. Vincent van Gogh said, "Your profession is not what brings home a paycheck. Your profession is what you are put here on earth to do with such passion that it becomes a spiritual calling."

To be a forward-thinking, forward-moving leader, you must continually stir your passions with the right thinking, the right doing and the right people around you. One of my mentors taught me the concept of going where you are celebrated NOT where you are merely tolerated.

When we surround ourselves with the right people, they will care about our success and push us to the next level through encouragement and honest feedback. Having the right people around you will also keep your passions stirred because like-minded people draw the best out of one another.

Willingness to Avoid Self-Righteousness

I was once a participant of a seminar in San Francisco, California, that I will never forget. We did one training "module" where we were eventually paired up with someone in the room who admittedly "had lots of negative judgment towards us." As about 80 of us stood in a circle, one of the facilitators asked a gentleman on the opposite side of the circle from me, whom he felt the most *negative judgment* towards. Like everyone else, I had no idea who he was going to choose. So, imagine my surprise when that six-foot-six giant (who happened to be a former professional football player) walked across the center of the circle and came to stand right in front of me. As if that weren't shocking enough, I was blown away when the facilitator asked the football player why he felt such judgment toward me. The man replied, "He's too self-righteous."

This began a relationship between the giant and I that revealed some pretty amazing things. The first of which was, we both carried an air of "self-righteousness." And just to be clear, I'm not talking about the kind of "self-righteousness" that people respect. This is the type of "self-righteousness" that people actually despise. It's the kind of "being-ness" that creates a wall between an individual and other people because the individual believes he or she is superior to someone else. "Self-righteousness" is a false sense of superiority that is often displayed through a subtle, condescending and entitled nature. And, the worst part is that the people who possess it, and in this case it was myself, are typically blind to it.

As a result of experiencing that valuable feedback from someone that I may have otherwise overlooked, I have been able to work on this specific area of my life, and it has helped me to be more effective when working with others. We may have respect for a person's position of authority, but when he or she carries this "self-righteous" attitude, it doesn't inspire us to follow them, nor does it inspire us to perform at our highest level. An interesting thing about identifying negative judgments that we have toward others is that the thing we are judging in someone else is a reflection of where we are ourselves. Thus, that negative quality we see in others is often something that we need to work through in order to grow in capacity and maturity. When my buddy in that exercise saw "self-righteousness" in me, it was because he could identify with it on a personal level. If he hadn't recognized what he was looking at, he would have simply overlooked me. You may have heard it said before, "How we see others is typically more a reflection of who *we* are than who *they* are."

Here are a few things that a self-righteous attitude can cost us when it comes to our team or family:

- Collaboration
- Trust
- Motivation
- Promotion
- Progress
- Support
- Genuine Relationships
- Legacy

Since you're reading this book, I know that you want to be a great leader. I must tell you that becoming a great leader is not always easy, though. To truly look forward into the future and make the commitment to be better, we must be willing to open ourselves up to feedback and then use it to grow. As author John Maxwell says, "You either grow towards where you're headed or you're probably not headed anywhere."

Too many times, individuals arrive at some level of success in life and begin to develop a "self-righteous" attitude. They become delusional! They tell themselves that they've achieved enough, and as a result, they want to parade it around in everyone else's face. Personally, I am grateful to the mentors I have had who have given me insight into the cause of "self-righteousness"—and it's not the result of a genuine feeling of accomplishment, as most people would think. A "self-righteous" attitude is actually driven by a **need to feel superior**, which originates from feelings of **inadequacy**. You see, if I feel really confident in who I am, I don't need to try to convince you that I'm good enough, or that I have all the answers. I can simply be comfortable in my own skin knowing that I don't need to prove anything to anyone else.

The most influential leaders **are** comfortable in their own skin. They have confidence and clarity, not insecurity and inferiority. And when you have a clear understanding of how people see you, you can begin to work on some of the blind spots that you may have developed throughout your life.

Being a part of a team that can speak openly and honestly will inevitably lead to growth for everyone involved **IF** feedback is shared with **honor and respect**. So, if you think that you may be struggling with a bit of self-righteousness, or if you have feelings of inferiority, talk to someone you **trust.** Ask that person what areas of your life you can improve on and then be willing to **do the work.** At first it might hurt a bit to hear the feedback, but as you work on these areas, you will gain more and more self-confidence and a more positive self-image. And when we feel good about ourselves, we do not need to project our superiority to anyone. We can simply meet people right where they are and lead them toward a desired organizational goal.

Consistency

The next quality of a forward-thinking leader is consistency. To build a better tomorrow, we must commit to being more consistent. I have heard it said, "What we do daily we become permanently."

So many dreams have been left unfulfilled because of a lack of consistency. Achieving your life's purpose is not about talent, and it's not about talk. It's about doing the small things daily that will lead to big outcomes. At the beginning of each day, we should begin the process of checking items off of our personal success list.

I recently traveled to Phoenix, Arizona, where I spoke to a group of realtors from Keller-Williams Realty. Keller-Williams is now on of the largest real estate agencies in the world. The company has achieved phenomenal success due to the forward thinking of Gary Keller, it's founder and CEO. Gary says in his book, *The One Thing*, that we don't need a to-do list; we need a **success** list. He says that to-do lists are often LONG, but success lists are SHORT. So, we need to identify the "one thing" that will bring us the best return on our time investment and consistently work toward that.

Far too many people major in minor things and wind up getting distracted by their day-to-day activities. As a result, they do not contribute to their own future success. Maybe it's checking your email. Maybe it's talking to friends. It could be social media, daydreaming, or it could be that you spend much of your valuable time watching television.

If we don't identify the things that are distracting us on a day-to-day basis, we're likely to continue doing them. We allow these distractions to fall into a category of things that we believe are permissible or even necessary. The most successful people I work with guard their creative energy and time as if those two things are the most important things in the world. When it comes to forward-thinking leadership, they actually *ARE*. People and activities can distract and drain us if we're not careful, and the higher we go on the ladder of success, the better we have to get at saying "no" to opportunities. As I said earlier in this book, "Success starts with a "YES" but is maintained by our willingness to say "NO."

Boundaries that we establish are blessings. To remain consistent, we must learn to say "no" to distractions. We must have the discipline and clarity for our future to be able to identify the things that are taking our attention. Here's a perspective that may help you: Think of the people in your future that you are actually "TAKING" from by not getting focused and producing your best results. Take a farmer, for example. Can you imagine how others would be affected if the farmer were too distracted during planting season to plant the seeds that were necessary for the harvest? Harvest time would roll around and there would be no crops for people to live on. As a leader, we must be consistent when it comes to doing the RIGHT things at the RIGHT time.

When we're consistent, clear-minded and committed, we create strong results. But when we are casual, we create problems. I've always said that **casualness breeds casualties**. Therefore, our goals for tomorrow and our hopes for the future could die if we don't develop the consistency that is going to produce the right results. I like to think of this as having a "Spirit of Excellence." Excellence is not a one-time act; it's actually a lifestyle. Forward-thinking leaders understand this, and they approach their jobs, businesses, family and other areas of their life with a spirit of excellence and determination. From that place, they develop the consistent habits that lead to this lifestyle that will, in turn, help everyone to win. Maybe, up until this point, you haven't been very consistent regarding the important things in your life. The good news is that today is an amazing place to start. Are you going to continue to say, "One Day" or are you going to start saying "Day One?" This moment can be the beginning of a better life if you will decide that today is "Day One" and get to work developing better habits.

Boldness

The last quality I would like to mention here of forward-thinking leaders is boldness. The Webster's Dictionary defines boldness as: "Showing ability to take risks; confident; and courageous." When we think of people who represent the courage required for boldness, we often think of soldiers, firemen and police officers serving their communities. Or, we may think of iconic figures like Muhammad Ali, Walt Disney, Henry David Thoreau, Jackie Robinson and Billy Graham. These individuals exhibited the boldness necessary to impact masses of people and even transform entire industries. They possessed the courage and willingness to think, speak and act differently than the majority of the people of their time.

Courage doesn't have to make a big scene, and I believe some of the most courageous decisions of our life are often unseen. When someone faces a personal fear and chooses to take action anyway, that is courage. Likewise, it takes true courage to be bold in a world that stresses the importance of fitting in. Conformity and casualness are the offspring of a culture that emphasizes the need for majority acceptance. If the next generations are not careful, they will lose their voice in a sea of noise, being led astray by an abundance of sounds created by a world screaming for attention. It is bold leaders who instill values of courage into those who will follow, and who will speak up for those who may not have a voice.

The participants of NASA's lion program are bold leaders who are moving into greater positions of leadership and influence every day. These rising leaders are doing so within an organization that continually stretches the boundaries of what's possible. We can all take our rightful position as leaders in the world this exact same way if we are willing to accept the role. It takes boldness to get up each day and stand for something that you believe in. It takes boldness to speak truth when it might be easier to sit amongst a lie. It takes boldness to fight for our families and for our planet.

When we see many of the images of astronauts in outer space smiling and floating in zero gravity, we often forget that to get to outer space, they had to ride a rocket that burned close to half a million gallons of fuel to escape the Earth's atmosphere. In other words, they sat atop a controlled explosion. That's boldness!

Just because we feel anxious or think people may ridicule us, doesn't mean we don't still have the responsibility to be leaders in our world. Yes, we may try and then fail, but boldness is what it takes to even make the attempt. In a board meeting, the courage to speak up about challenges, instead of trying to avoid stepping on anyone's toes, is a sign of a bold leader. It also takes boldness to have tough conversations with your spouse or with your children - but it beats keeping secrets that can destroy the fabric of your family. I've seen too many people who would not boldly step into a place of vulnerability and authenticity, and, as a result, now look back on their life with regret as some of their most important relationships were allowed to fall apart.

When we choose to be bold, we are willing to do what others might not be willing to do; to say what others might not say; and to stand when others might not stand. What will you stand for today? Will you stand for yourself and for others? Will you stand for your values and for the mission of your family and team? Will you stand for leaving a legacy that can never be erased? Or will you sit back and just let things happen? It's all up to you! I know boldness isn't always easy, but I know that it is always worth it. Be bold.

CHAPTER 7

Dream Impossible Dreams

"*The world is a dangerous place. Not because of those who do evil, but because of those who look on and do nothing.*"

Albert Einstein

When the Voyager probes were launched by NASA in 1977, they were sent with greetings from Earth just in case they encountered any alien life-forms as they made their long journey through the universe. These greetings were sent via gold-plated discs that could play both sounds and images and featured greetings in 55 different languages, pictures of life on Earth, and information about where the probes came from. These records were compiled by some of the world's most brilliant scientists - people who believe that life probably exists somewhere else in the universe. As one scientist put it, "If there's not life out there, it's a terrible waste of space."

****

As we consider the tremendous accomplishments of our nation's space program in just the last 50 years, have you thought about the fact that around a hundred years ago humans were still using horse and buggy as their primary mode of transportation? Have you also considered that airplanes were non-existent during that time? When we consider these things, we realize just how much we have changed and grown in the past century, as well as the potential of where we could be in just one century more.

Right now, NASA is about to begin testing it's SLS, or Space Launch Systems, as the first phase of the mission to Mars. The mission to Mars will mean sending astronauts to set foot on a planet over a hundred million miles away. The technology, planning, and procedures that will be required to pull off this accomplishment are mind-blowing. And it will happen!

It is believed that the Milky Way galaxy has over four hundred billion stars. It is also believed that there are more than four hundred billion galaxies in the known universe. So when we truly consider this, we can see why NASA would send out probes, along with an attempt to communicate with anyone who might one day encounter them.

But if the question, "Are we alone in the universe?" scares you, or if you immediately jump to conclusions based on what you think you know, it's possible that you're falling victim to, and making decisions based on, the limited knowledge that you have now.

We all have a deep need for certainty, even if our certainty is based on old information. To combat this trap, I want to discuss the importance of continuing to pursue more knowledge and embrace the possibilities of what could be. By jumping to a conclusion or deciding that it's best to not think about such extreme possibilities, we actually limit what is available to us.

This is not about convincing you that there are aliens in outer space. I just hope that, for the sake of your own leadership and influence in the future, you will keep an open mind - not just to the possibility of alien life, but to any other possibility that may cross your path. I believe that keeping an open mind is one of the greatest requirements for being effective and influential in the future. Unfortunately, our tendency is often to default to what we already believe, because breaking out of an old paradigm can be scary and extremely uncomfortable. We often find peace of mind in going back to information that we were told years ago - even decades ago - by people that had limited information and insight.

Your influence on the generations to come will be in direct proportion to your willingness to see things from a new perspective while admitting that you don't have all the answers. Sometimes this type of thinking is seen as "the rabbit trail of life, going down a path to which there is no end." I see it as our greatest responsibility! Why on earth would we settle for the limited information that we have and use it to conclude that our own existence here is to simply follow old rules that were created with old mindsets?

I believe that it's the people who "pretend" to have all the answers that secretly want to use their false certainty to keep the rest of us doubting ourselves. If someone can confuse you, or convince you to doubt your own abilities, they take away the very thing that makes you who you are. When we know who we are, and are unwilling to compromise for anyone or anything, the possibilities for our future impact becomes unlimited. Otherwise, we are confined by the limitations that someone else has created for us.

Marianne Williamson said, "The opportunities for infinite possibility exist, no matter what age we might be." Giving ourselves permission to think on the impossible, we often bump up against barriers that we, or someone else, may have already constructed. As a child, we're always looking; we're always learning; and we're always growing. But, as we get older, *we're always judging; we're always reconsidering; and we're always settling for what we think we know.* This is one of our biggest problems. Dwelling in the place of possibility for yourself, your family, and your life, gives you the power to create anything that you can imagine. In order to create something that has never been created, we must first allow ourselves to imagine such a thing. Impossibilities cannot exist within the realm of preconceived notions.

Friedrich Nietzsche said, "A thought, even a possibility, can shatter and transform us." When was the last time you allowed yourself to have a new thought that could radically shape who you believe you could become? It likely stems from something or someone in your past. Right now, who you believe you are currently is comprised of the labels you have placed on yourself with a perspective that you've already had. In other words, you believe you are who you are based on a decision you made in the past. Truthfully, each day carries the possibility of new labels, new insight, and new opportunity. *We must be careful not to use the old labels to determine what new labels we should even consider.*

What if, starting today, you decided that you would no longer resort to previous labels or consider your past when you begin to visualize your future? Maybe it's a new career, new relationship, home in a new city; maybe it's a brand-new self-image. What if you realized today that you were free to become anything that you wished to become? It's from this place that you become powerful. Without that, you're simply living within false, preconceived limitations. This is not to say that we should completely abandon the life that we've worked hard to create. But, I believe that becoming a bold, courageous, LION leader means that we must be willing to push the limits further than we are typically comfortable with, and let go of the thinking that we've been holding onto for so long.

Muhammad Ali once said, "Impossible is just a big word thrown around by small men who find it easier to live in a world they've been given, rather than explore the power that they have to change it. Impossible is not a fact, it's an opinion. Impossible is not a declaration, it's a dare. Impossible is potential. Impossible is temporary. Impossible is nothing."

On May 6th, 1954, Roger Bannister broke what many believed to be an impossible barrier: the four-minute mile.

Oddly enough, as soon as it was broken, many athletes followed suit, and since then, the mile record has been lowered by 17 seconds. We typically only push ourselves toward something that we believe is possible for us. However, history shows that when one person steps up their efforts, it creates the space for many others to do the same. What have you decided is your limitation when it comes to income, relationship, influence and physical health?

Right now, you may be thinking, "Ronnie, I know there are no limits." But unconsciously, you haven't set a big enough goal to come face-to-face with what it is that you *REALLY* believe. By not setting big goals, you have already unconsciously decided that you will never achieve more than what is normal for you. And, if that's okay with you, it's okay with me. I'm not here to tell you how to live! I'm only here to provoke your thinking in such a way that you expand your vision—not only for yourself, but also for those who might be following you. Think of Roger Bannister and then think of all the young athletes who must have looked up to him. Because of his accomplishments, they were willing to say, "I want to do that." Think of the hours of practice and training that they put in, simply because they believed that they also could run a four-minute mile.

How we choose to move creates space for others to follow. Do you realize that one single conversation, one single act, and even a single thought, can begin to change the direction of where you're headed in life? What if today you decided to do one thing - something that wasn't even in your comfort zone - and then monitored how that decision would affect your mindset and mood? What if you took a test drive in a new luxury car, or drove into a neighborhood with multi million-dollar homes? What if you signed up to learn martial arts, or take dance classes? What if you simply made the decision to reinvent yourself? There's nothing wrong with how you are but by breaking the patterns of what is normal in your life, you may begin to experience much more than what you have currently settled for.

All astronauts share about the first time they reached outer space and were able to look back on our planet. Almost always, they talk about how their mindset immediately shifted from borders and limitations to inclusion and infinite possibility. Once your mind has been stretched, it can never go back to its original size. So after finishing this book, what practices will you add to your life that will stretch you like never before?

Are you willing to create a vision board filled with things

that you would love to do and places that you would love to visit? Are you willing to set bigger goals than you already have and ask someone for support and accountability? These questions may cause you to squirm a bit as you realize that you'll have to get outside your comfort zone to make them happen. But as Colin Powell said, "A dream doesn't become reality by magic; it takes sweat, determination, and hard work."

The Fear of Dreaming

I believe the dreams that we are willing to pursue can give us a wonderful road map to follow as we move through this journey called life. If we are afraid to dream, then essentially, we're afraid to live. Dreams give us direction to move forward and help us determine our priorities. Dreams give us passion! They also give us initiative while unlocking an unknown future. And the best thing about our dreams is that, at any moment of the day, we can decide to pursue them with all our heart. Unfortunately many of us have stopped dreaming for the following reasons:

- Dreaming costs us nothing, and what we give nothing for, we do not value.

Because using our imagination to dream costs us nothing, we often take our imagination for granted and stop using it to the extent that we could. We often place our imagination on the back burner in our mind and only focus on the life that is playing out in front of our eyes.

- A dream carries with it a choice: the choice to take action or to stay the same.

When we refuse to do anything with our dreams for prolonged periods of time, we tend to fall into a frustrated state of mind. This frustrated state of mind can make it more challenging to dream inspiring dreams.

- Dreams can be uncomfortable.

Dreams have the potential to destroy paradigms that have been established in our subconscious mind. When we begin to dream and set big goals, it can trigger feelings of nervousness and anxiety. As a result, many people sink back into their comfort zone that eventually leads to mediocrity.

- Past dreams may not have come true.

One of my favorite quotes is this: "Don't complain

about the results you didn't get from the work you were unwilling to do." When we are honest about our shortcomings, we can acknowledge the fact that our dreams may not have come true simply because we didn't work hard enough. Remember, dreams do not occur by magic. We must be willing to cover ourselves in sweat and do the work necessary to see our dreams come to pass.

We MUST dare to dream AGAIN!

Regardless of the circumstances that may have caused you to stop dreaming, I believe that, as a LION leader, you must be willing to dream again. Here's why:

Without a dream, you will never work harder for anything more than what you ALREADY have in front of you.

There are many people who have made a habit of looking down to see the path that lies beneath them, while forgetting that the key to seeing further is simply a willingness to look up. Each week I take time to look up at the stars in the universe and think about things that could possibly exist beyond what I see with my naked eye. It's in these moments that I ask myself what could lie beyond what I already see that could change what I believe. I consider this same type of thinking when I consider my goals. I believe that we must create "the horizon beyond the horizon" if we want to ensure that we achieve significant goals. If we dream bigger and set bigger goals, we can then pass through the goal, not just arrive at it.

The goal beyond the goal is an almost sure way for us to achieve the initial goal. Norman Vincent Peale said, "Aim for the moon, if you miss it at least you will wind up in the stars."

We must dream as a repayment for those who gave their lives for us to be able to dream.

If you're reading this book right now, I know that you're free. You're free to read what you want, say what you want, and ultimately, do what you want. People have literally fought and died to give us those freedoms! So, wouldn't their sacrifices be rewarded better if we chose to do all that we could do with the freedoms they provided? I know that if you were in a position in which you were fighting for the freedom of future generations, you would hope that none of those individuals would take your efforts for granted. I recently heard a quote that said, "If you take the things you've been given for granted, the things that you've been given get taken."

We must dream again because remaining the same will lead to sad outcomes in the future for the inhabitants of Earth.

If we do not dream of new ways to improve the environment and replenish natural resources, generations to come will have to live with the circumstances that we are now creating. Dreaming can stir our passions, clarify our priorities, and push us to do more than we have in the past to leave a better tomorrow for those to come. I am often frustrated when I hear people talking about how they are going to fly away to the afterlife and as a result are unconcerned with the future of our planet.

This "escapism" mindset can cause the next generation to have to deal with issues that we as leaders could have solved. My mother always told me to "Leave things better than you found it." I plan on using that advice when it comes to how I have lived on this planet.

Dreaming inspires others to dream

Just as Roger Bannister inspired others, how we choose to dream will motivate those who look to us for inspiration. Imagine the possibilities of a world filled with people who were not glued to their smart devices, but who actually utilized their time to dream and create. Billions of man-hours a year could be used to correct some of the challenges that have been created throughout past generations, or to create new technologies that could further transform and improve life as we know it. I always say, "be picky with your dreams, your friends and your time." Don't be afraid to look at your goals and dreams and be willing to stretch them to new levels. They may call us dreamers but we are not the ones who are asleep! If you only get one thing from this book that you are reading, I hope that you will see that I believe it's the dreamers that will change our world. Don't be afraid to dream!

Now, let's take a look at what has been achieved regarding our universe and space travel by individuals who have dared to **DREAM BIG:**

- In 1609, Galileo perfected his telescope and used it to prove that planets revolve around the sun, and not the other way around.

- In 1682, Edmund Halley tracked a comet and determined that it made an appearance approximately every 76 years, concluding it must be orbiting the sun. Then, when it re-appeared on schedule in 1758, it was named Halley's Comet.

- In 1926 Robert Goddard, an American scientist, launched the first modern rocket using liquid fuel, which paved the way for modern space travel.

- In 1957 the Soviets launched Sputnik 1, which was the first spaceship in space.

- In 1962, John Glenn became the first American to orbit the Earth when he circled the planet three times in less than five hours.

- In 1969 Neil Armstrong set foot on the moon.

- In 1972 NASA launched two Pioneer probes that were the first spacecraft to travel through the asteroid belt between Mars and Jupiter.

- In 1981 NASA launched the first space shuttle, Columbia, which carried 10 astronauts into space, stayed a week, and then returned to Earth.

- In 1990, the Hubble Telescope was launched.

- In 1994, work on the International Space Station began.

- In 1998 John Glenn became the oldest person in space, at the age of 77.

- In 2010, space shuttle Discovery returned to space for 10 days, and for the first time had four women in space together.

- On November 26th, 2011, Curiosity Rover was launched into space, beginning its journey towards Mars.

- Nine months later, on August 6th, 2012, the Rover landed in what is known as the Gale Crater on Mars. It currently navigates the Red Plant, studying its environment and habitability.

- On March 1st, 2016, astronaut Scott Kelly returned to Earth after spending a record 340 consecutive days in space aboard the International Space Station.

Thankfully, the individuals and organizations that I just mentioned did not take their ability to dream for granted. Instead, they used their dreams to fuel progress for all mankind. And though it's easy to speed through this list of accomplishments, it should be noted that making these things happen was no easy task. Each of these accomplishments were the result of a dreamer dreaming -

and then being willing to do the work necessary to see it through.

Regardless of your past or how you may have failed, I dare you to dream. If you truly believe that this is the only life that you're going to live, you owe it to yourself to dream again.

Dreaming, Defined

When I think about the word "dream," spelled D-R-E-A-M, it has a special meaning to me:

D stands for DECISION

We must make the decision that, regardless of where we have come from, the challenges that we have faced, and the people that have walked out of our life, we must decide to begin AGAIN. No one who has ever changed the world did so without massive resistance, and though they may not have realized it at the time, the pain of resistance made them stronger than they would have been otherwise.

In spite of this resistance, you must decide to fight again. When you make the decision to begin again, you will wake each day with a new passion and eagerness to see how your life can unfold. And simply deciding that we're going to push on, regardless of the circumstances, actually causes us to tap into the infinite source that I call God - at which point miracles begin to happen. Decisions are the precipitator for change! But without an intentional decision, the change we experience will be less than what could have been our best. Remember: In the beginning, we make our decisions, but in the end, our decisions make us.

R stands for RESOLVE

You must resolve to never quit. The graveyard is full of individuals with unfulfilled hopes and dreams. Every person on this planet has a dream for something, but very, very few will actually pursue it. The only thing that lies between you and your dream is the excuse that you have created, and the story that you tell yourself to affirm it. We must confront our lies, our excuses, and our self-imposed limitations, and forge ahead trusting that when we do our part, the universe will respond. Whether in sickness or pain, in difficulty or challenge, we must resolve to lift our chin, pull our shoulders back, and press forward to the higher calling that has been placed within us. When we resolve to push until we become powerful; when we resolve to fight until we cannot lose; when we resolve to honor our deepest passion with unrelenting action, we conquer.

E stands for ENGAGE

Engage innovative ideas. Throw everything on the table! Think of no idea as silly or unnecessary. Engage the insight of a trusted mentor. Engage feedback. In doing so, you will find that what may hurt your pride today can be the best thing for you in the future. Engage in uplifting and progressive dialogue. If you only speak with those who have achieved the same level of success as you, you won't learn the principles necessary to take you to the next level. And lastly, engage in prayer. Regardless of your spiritual views, connecting with the Creator of the universe is one of the most important things that you can do. Prayer gives me peace, and from that peace I am much more creative.

A stands for ASK

Ask yourself TOUGH questions. Those who are afraid to ask will be controlled by what they've already been told. On the contrary, asking unlocks the door for deeper understanding. When you refuse to ask, you're actually refusing to change. We can never grow to a place that we aren't first aware exists. Asking questions can shed light on areas where our deepest understanding may be in the dark. Asking shows our desire for knowledge. Ask yourself if what you believe is absolutely true, or if you have adopted it as "truth" because you simply haven't been willing to search any further?

M stands for MASTER THE MOMENTS

Our entire life is made up of individual moments. These moments give us the opportunity to choose and re-choose again. Every moment is rich with the potential to change the trajectory of our life. Mastering the moments means mastering your impulses and the thoughts that drive your feelings.

When we master the enemy within, the one on the outside can do us no harm! When we master our mouth, we take account for the words that we speak about our families, our teams, goals and our current situations. When we master our skills - in whatever we choose to do - we begin to do it to the best of our abilities with all our heart even on the days we might not feel like it.

Finally, when we master our heart, we guard it, we

protect it, and we nurture it with wisdom and truth. Out of our heart flow the issues of life. Our heart gives us the rhythm by which we live our lives. When we live from our heart, we experience more love, more joy, and more compassion than those who refuse to open up to our world. Mastering the moments by slowing down, taking a deep breath, noticing your surroundings and being present, are just a few of the keys to mastering your life. Don't be in such a hurry to get somewhere that you never spend any time being somewhere. The place is right where you are and the time is now!

The Costs of Non-Existent Dreams

Your dreams do not have an expiration date! So, take this moment to decide to begin again. I am not a person who offers many guarantees in life, but if you refuse to allow yourself to dream again, I can guarantee you that you will experience some of the following things:

Regret

I would much rather deal with the pain of disappointment and discomfort than the pain of regret. Pain is temporary; regret is permanent. You will regret the chances that you did not take and the opportunities that you did not pursue- maybe not today and maybe not tomorrow, but soon, and for the rest of your life.

Mediocrity

If you do not dream, I can guarantee you that you'll eventually have to settle for a life that is far less than what it could have been. Settling for less means that those you could have passed the "baton of legacy" to will have to experience less as well. Without dreaming, you will lack the fire and passion to set others' dreams ablaze. When we set ourselves on fire with the passion to achieve more, others are warmed from the heat and they use that flame to help light their path as they move toward their next level.

Negative Impact

I can guarantee you that if you do not dream, others will be negatively impacted! Whether you think your dreams matter or not, please recognize that other people's dreams do. Someone may need YOU to show them the way toward an extraordinary life. Since we know that there are people watching us and waiting to follow, a great question to ask is,

"Where am I leading people?" If we choose the path of least resistance, we arrive at a destination called "Average." But, if we push through the resistance and keep our eyes on the mountaintop, we will undoubtedly arrive at a place called "Amazing."

With every step that we're willing to take off of the beaten path, we make a way for those that follow to make greater progress. When I am dreaming, I often picture a young person who I have mentored growing up to impact the world. I then imagine that person saying to me, "Thank you! Thank you for giving me the confidence to never quit, to go after my dreams, and to achieve them."

What higher compliment could we ever receive than that?

Whether you believe others are watching you or not, and whether you see yourself as a leader or not, I hope that you know this: <u>You are worth the sacrifice</u>. Your value is not wrapped up in how others see you, but in how you choose to see yourself. When you see yourself as powerful, beautiful, and a creation that can continually impact the world in a positive way, you will find the motivation and inspiration to push ahead. No, every day won't be easy, and some days you will feel like you're not making progress at all. But with each new day comes a new set of possibilities to have what others won't have, and encounter what you have not yet encountered. Regardless of those who may have tried to get you to give up on your dreams or to give up on yourself; regardless of those who may have assigned false motives to you and said hateful things about you; and regardless of what didn't work out in the past, you must continue to dream. If not for you, then for all of us. Albert Einstein said, "The world is a dangerous place. Not because of those who do evil, but because of those who look on and do nothing."

I know that you would never intentionally do harm to another human being, but unintentionally, I believe that we can do it every day. Whether it's starvation in third-world countries or the lack of clean drinking water, many people are paying for our choices. Being a true LION leader means we willfully accept the responsibilities to do our part by becoming our best and giving our best. Not only for our hopes and our dreams but also for the hopes and the dreams of others.

In our nation alone, one in 45 children are homeless. The idea that some lives matter less than others is the root of all that is wrong with the world that we live in. LION leaders know that we are all created equally. When the power of love overcomes the love of power, the world will know peace.

President John F. Kennedy once said, "We stand today on the edge of a new frontier, a frontier of unknown opportunities and perils, a frontier of unfulfilled hopes and threats." Even though he uttered those words over 50 years ago, much of what he said still rings true today. Whether it's the threat of terrorism, disease, or war, each of us has the responsibility to stand against these threats and live in such a way to keep freedom alive, not only for us, but for many generations to come. And it all starts with our willingness to dream impossible dreams.

CHAPTER 8

Be the Teammate You Want to Have

"It was pride that changed angels to devils, and it's humility that makes men as angels."

Saint Augustine

One of NASA's most well known teams is the crew of Apollo 13. The three-astronaut crew made history in 1970 when they barely made it back to earth after a chain of nearly catastrophic events while on their mission in outer space. The story was so incredible that an award-winning movie starring Tom Hanks, Kevin Bacon, and Ed Harris, directed by Ron Howard, was made about it years later.

The Apollo 13 mission was commanded by James Lovell, Jack Swigert, and Fred Haise. Gene Kranz was the lead flight director at mission control during that now-famous mission. He was on the other end of the conversation when the phrase, "Houston, we've had a problem," was first uttered. An explosion inside the oxygen tanks onboard had rendered the service module useless. As a result, intense conditions ensued within the command module. Limited power, loss of heat, shortage of water, and the buildup of deadly carbon dioxide became issues that seemed almost insurmountable for the crew as they floated in outer space. Despite the harsh conditions, however, the crew was able to return back to Earth five days later, on April 17th, 1970. The safe return of the mission was called nothing short of a miracle.

That miracle was attributed to the human factor back here on Earth. Gene Kranz, lead flight director, said the blend of young, intelligent minds, working day in and day out - by sheer willpower - had yielded the right stuff. This commitment to leadership and persistence had been forged only a few years earlier after the failed NASA mission of Apollo 1, during which astronauts Ed White, Gus Grissom, and Roger Chaffee were killed in an explosion on the launch pad. The Monday following the tragic events of Apollo 1, Gene Kranz called a meeting of his branch in flight control team to express his values and admonishments for future space flight at NASA.

The Kranz Dictum, as it is now called, exemplifies the

foundational values of teamwork that NASA is now known for. In that meeting, Kranz delivered the following message:

"Space flight will never tolerate casualness, incapacity or neglect. Somewhere, somehow, we've screwed up. It could have been in design, build, or test. Whatever it was, we should have caught it. We were too gung-ho about the schedule, and we locked out all the problems that we saw in our day-to-day work. Every element of the program was in trouble, and so were we. The simulators were not working. Mission control was behind in virtually every area, and the flight and test procedures changed daily. Nothing we did had any shelf life. Not one of us stood up and said, 'Stop.'

I don't know what Thompson's committee will find as the cause, but I know what I find. We are the cause. We were not ready. We did not do our job. We were rolling the dice, hoping that things would come together by launch day, when in our hearts we knew it would take a miracle. From this day forward, flight control will be known by two words: 'tough' and 'competent.'

Tough means we are forever accountable for what we do, or for what we fail to do. We will never again compromise our responsibilities. Every time we walk into Mission Control, we will know what we stand for.

Competent means we will never take anything for granted. We will never be found short in our knowledge and in our skills. Mission Control will be perfect.

When you leave this meeting today, you will go to your office and write two words on your blackboards: the words are 'tough' and 'competent.' It must never be erased. Each day when you enter the room, those words will remind you of the price paid by Grissom, White, and Chaffee. These words are the price of admission to the ranks of our Mission Control."

"Tough and competent," as Kranz stated, are the qualities that I believe set the context for why the Apollo 13 mission was able to overcome the huge challenges that it faced only three years later. When a team decides that no matter what the circumstances, and no matter what the challenges, they will overcome - miracles happen. By setting the very context for success, teamwork is then fueled, and the results are astounding. All great teams stand by a similar commitment, and as a result, the players on the team are able to grow into their greatness.

I want to take this time to discuss building teams. Building teams is an essential skill for any great leader. After reading the following, I hope you will understand the importance of having a great team around you. When you are willing to face some of your own beliefs and prejudices and step into a new level of boldness, courage and authenticity, you will naturally identify the right people for your teams.

One of my beliefs, when it comes to having the right people around you, is this: Not everyone that is with you is for you, and not everyone that is for you is with you. I also don't believe that people are necessarily against us. I just believe that they are really, really for themselves. Having the right team around you requires self-reflection, as well as dedication. You must BECOME the team player that you want to have on your team!

Here are four things that I believe are required to become a great team player.

Vision

Number one, great team players have a clear VISION of what victory will look like. You've probably heard it said, "Without vision, people perish." Vision is the precursor of commitment because we must first know what it is that we want to accomplish before we can ever make it happen. The clarity of our vision will then help to fuel the passions that are necessary to push through the challenges that will come as we pursue success. As our passions align with those of other like-minded individuals, we can then make an absolute commitment to the desired outcome of the team. As we commit to the team's success, we are committed to the processes that will make the team successful. As a result, we must move our own personal desires to the back burner so that the overall best for the team can move forward.

Even though putting our own personal interest aside is tough at times, it is truly where the opportunities for growth and success lie. Pat Riley, former coach of the world champion Los Angeles Lakers, said, "The disease of ME, if untreated, leads to the defeat of US." I believe this quote exemplifies the importance of choosing to serve rather than be served. When we focus on ourselves, we are limited. But when we can add our talents, values and commitment to a large, unified body, our potential grows exponentially. Vision - for ourselves and for the team—is the key to making this happen.

Communication

Great team players know that without strong communication, strong execution is next to impossible. Great teams communicate openly, honestly, and responsibly.

Great team players understand, as Susan Scott said in her book *Fierce Leadership*, that "what gets talked about and how it gets talked about determines what will happen in an organization." In short, our words are powerful and we must use them well! The late Jim Rohn used to say, "Never get lazy with your language, because words are far too important." I've heard others say that words are weapons, and we either use them to defeat our enemies or defeat ourselves.

In an organization or even a family, gossip is deadly. People who are divisive and speak negative things about the team can destroy the potential for victory. In contrast, a willingness to be open and honest - in a responsible way - leads members of the team or family to feel empowered, as opposed to feeling oppressed. Creative energy can then flow, versus negative energy taking over. If we're frustrated with something, a willingness to check our motives, do some detective work, and allow patience to have her perfect work can lead to having better, more fruitful conversations and build trust within the team.

So remember, be open and be honest, but also be responsible for your feelings. When we carefully use the proper framework for our communication, we can share our thoughts and feeling without causing other people to feel attacked. LION leaders always use their words in skillful and intentional way without doing harm to those that hear. Be bold enough to communicate honestly but while doing it with honor and compassion.

Humility

The next quality of a great team player is HUMILITY. Some of the most powerful people that I know are the most humble when it comes to leadership and influence. And just for clarity, humility doesn't mean that you walk around acting like you've been humiliated. Tariq Ramadan, Swiss philosopher, said this regarding humility: "Clarity and consistency are not enough. The quest for truth requires humility as well as effort." And Saint Augustine said, "It was pride that changed angels to devils, and it's humility that makes men as angels." There are few compliments that I believe we can be given that are greater than being called "humble."

My father, Ronnie Doss Sr., whom I am still very close to, was a brick mason from the small town of Mount Airy, North Carolina. Growing up, I saw how my father treated people. He always had a kind word of encouragement for them. When he was complimented on his family or his work, he would always reply with such warmth and kindness. He seemed to always be thankful for the opportunity to work and serve his community with his talent of brick masonry. To this day, I can still drive back to North Carolina and see the homes in our small town that he built over 30 years ago. Because of my father's disciplined work ethic and kindness, he made a lasting impact on others as well as myself.

Maya Angelou said, "People will forget what you say, but they will never forget how you made them feel." So as we work with the individuals on our teams, we have an opportunity to add to their confidence and their joy.

When we are humble, we are open to learning new things. And with these new things, we add value to ourselves in the marketplace. It's said that "we don't get paid for our time; we get paid for the value that we bring to the time." Our willingness to add value to ourselves and the team will be directly related to our willingness to get past some of our own self-centered attitudes. If we believe that we are the center of it all, and that our personal needs are always more important that that of a team, we won't be a great team player.

Instead, as a team player - and leader - we can allow humility to tell us that we are all created equally, and that no one is better than anyone else. Whether someone is higher or lower than us on the organizational chart, they deserve to be respected. No matter what our position, when we can serve other people with honor and respect, it truly opens the door for us to gain favor with them and lead them to the next level. When we go from "working for a position" to "working for the team," we become powerful. Humble yourself and SERVE.

Commitment

The fourth quality of a great team player is COMMITMENT. In fact, the simple truth that we don't get what we want, we get what we are committed to, has impacted the way I approach every day of my life. Whether it's relational or financial, my spiritual health or my physical health, I know that I don't achieve things because I want them, I achieve them when I am committed to them.

I learned this truth about commitment almost a decade ago, and since then I have asked myself this question continually: Am I really committed to making great things happen, or do I just *want* great things to happen? This question helps me in my day-to-day choices as it pertains to my goals. As you know by now, I believe that goals are an important part of life. We can use our goals as the necessary benchmarks to measure our progress. If we don't believe that we are making progress toward something greater than where we already are, hopelessness can quickly set in. When we decide to commit to a goal, a purpose, or a dream that is greater than where we already are, an important part of our mind is activated. When we set a goal outside of our current reality, we activate the part of our mind known as the CREATIVE UNCONSCIOUS. The creative unconscious then provokes other parts of our mind to seek out the resources necessary to aid in our commitment to success.

Unfortunately, few people really understand how commitment actually works. So with that in mind, I want to share four commitment principles that I have learned with you.

Commitment Principle #1: Our commitments equal our results.

This may be the most profoundly powerful statement that I've ever adopted in my life. By understanding what commitment truly is, we can then start to investigate deeper commitments and see why we are producing some of the results we are. As an example, a man may say he is committed to a strong marriage. But, if he constantly demeans and disrespects his wife, he may be more deeply committed to manipulation and control.

One of the words my mentor, Mr. Klemmer, used to describe a person's deepest commitment was "INTENTION." He would ask, "Ronnie, what's your intention for this event?" With that question, he was basically asking me to be specific about the outcome I was committed to creating.

My job, as it pertained to the event, was to enroll people into my mentor's seminars by sharing insights regarding belief systems and problem solving. It was a great opportunity for me to see what I could create by getting clear on my INTENTION. By taking ownership of my intention and utilizing that ownership to help create the results that I wanted in my life. Knowing that the results I produce are not by accident - and that what I really, truly get committed to is what I will produce, has helped me to stay motivated, focused and more in control.

Commitment Principle #2: When the INTENTION is clear, the way will appear.

This principle has helped me to focus on what I'm

actually committed to. I have seen time and time again that when someone is truly committed to making something happen, they'll find a way. And if they're not committed, they will find an excuse.

Once in Kamloops, British Columbia, I had a flight scheduled at 6 a.m. to head back to the United States to speak at another event that evening. The morning I was to fly out, fog had covered the airport in Kamloops and delayed all the flights until later that afternoon. I was worried! The lady that had given me a ride to the airport had attended the event that I had spoken at the night before where I had talked about INTENTION. She could see that I was worried about not making the event, so she asked me, "Ronnie, what's your intention? Are you committed to making the event or not?"

I quickly did a self-check of my intentions at the moment, and I realized that I'd been more committed to being worried than I was to finding a solution. From there I made a quick shift, and I responded, "I am committed." She then said, "That's great! Now let's make it happen."

My friend then got on the phone, called a few of her friends and asked them to search for flights within a few hours' drive of Kamloops. It was 5 a.m. at the time and I didn't have a cell phone that worked outside the US. So, my friend was waking up her friends in the wee hours of the morning to ask them to support my new COMMITMENT.

Shortly thereafter, a few of her friends found flights. We gave one of them a credit card over the phone and they booked a flight in Kelowna, British Columbia for me. We then jumped back in the car and, in another twist of events, my friend took me to another friend's house because she was not able to drive me all the way to Kelowna herself. By the time we arrived at her friends house, her friend had already backed the car into the driveway and opened the trunk, ready for my bags. We loaded the bags into the trunk of the car and we headed off to catch a flight in Kelowna, British Columbia.

To make a really long story short, after riding in the car with this heavy-footed Canadian gentleman, I made it to the airport in just enough time to make the flight. I got to the States and walked onto the platform of my next even with only minutes to spare. It was a crazy, amazing day reminding me that all results begin with an intention AND that when our INTENTION is clear, the way will appear.

Here's a terrific question to ask yourself in regards to your future: Are you committed to producing the results that you say that you want, or will you be more committed to quitting when the challenges appear?

Commitment Principle #3: There's an infinite number of mechanisms for any one INTENTION.

Understanding this principle gives us a broader perspective on how to solve problems. When I speak to groups, I'll ask, for example, "How many different ways are there to improve a marriage?" Of course, the participants will say that there are limitless ways. Yet when I ask if that is how our society typically thinks when faced with the typical marital pressures, their response is "No!"

You see, when we feel pressure in life, we'll typically do one of two things: We either step up and get committed to the result we want OR we step down and get committed to making our excuses right. WOW!

When we stop living from a place of probability and move to a place of possibility, as we have talked about already, a whole new world of endless options opens up to us. All the great inventors from our past knew this! They clearly understood that if you made something your INTENTION, stuck with it long enough, endured the disappointments, and stayed the course, the universe would eventually reveal something NEW. This is how inventions are invented!

So I ask: Do you believe in yourself? And do you believe that the universe will provide a way if you stay the course?

Taking ownership of these commitment principles will help you to lead with more boldness, self-confidence, and POWER. Otherwise, you will believe that there are always circumstances that will be stopping you, that you will always be a victim to those circumstances, and that you don't really have the power to create what you want. Either way, you are committed to something.

Commitment Principle #4: There will be competing commitments.

When we make a commitment toward a desired goal, there will always be other commitments that will try to fight against it. For example, when I'm committed to spending an hour a day writing in my journal or scripting out resources, if I allow someone to talk me into having coffee with them, my commitment to the relationship overpowers my commitment to writing. Much of the time, these competing commitments are neither right nor wrong. If I choose to go have coffee to nurture a friendship or build a business connection, that's not a wrong use of my time. However, if I have set a goal to release a new resource and I haven't completed the writing, being committed to coffee may not be the best use of my time!

At any given moment, the commitment you give the most energy to will win.

****

Whether you're a part of a family or business team, there's nothing more satisfying than achieving an organizational objective with the people you love doing life with. As we increase our capacity as a leader, by identifying what we are committed to, the influence we have with others will grow. I would recommend that you go back and re-read this past section on COMMITMENT. My life began to change the moment I decided to get committed to the things I wanted. When I lost my excuses, I found my results.

CHAPTER 9
Forge LION-Level Connections

"Teamwork begins with the building of trust, and the only way to do that is to overcome our need for invulnerability."

Patrick Lencioni

"One small step for man; one giant leap for mankind"

That phrase is known by millions and millions of people around the globe and it was spoken by a true LION leader. Before Neil Armstrong had ever become the first human to set foot on the moon, he had already considered time and time again what he would say if - and when - that incredible event occurred. Armstrong knew he wanted to fly at a very early age when he was introduced to it by his father. Then, at the age of fifteen he received his pilot's license, giving him the ability to fly a plane even before he could drive a car. His passion for flight later drove him to study aviation in college, and this infatuation was further fueled when the United States went to war with Korea.

At the conclusion of Armstrong's second year at Purdue University, his studies of aeronautical engineering were cut short as he left college to serve his country and become a pilot in the Korean War. By the age of 22, Armstrong had flown 78 missions and was known as a quick thinker with nerves of steel. He returned to Purdue at the end of the war, completing his degree and meeting his wife. Not many years later, Armstrong became a test pilot for some of the world's most technologically advanced aircraft. His ability to handle unfamiliar situations and scenarios while remaining calm is what took him to the top of his profession. Time and time again, his courage, bravery, and abilities were tested as he learned to maneuver aircraft in tough situations.

Perhaps even more important than Neil Armstrong's flying prowess is the fact that other pilots and astronauts remember him as a terrific team player. Neil exemplified humility and earned the trust of those on his team.

If you've ever visited the Redwood forest of California, you've no doubt marveled at the incredible Redwood trees that can grow to over 300 feet tall. The reason these trees can endure the test of time and grow to amazing heights is because their root systems are interlocking. These interlocking root systems help one another to stand tall and endure conditions that would have taken down any one tree standing on it's own.

Teamwork exists on this same principle: All of us, together, are far stronger than any of us separated. Each of us can look at our lives and see that it was during the tough times that we truly learned the importance of having others to lean on. It is often in the times when we have shed the most tears and relied on the support of others that we have had the clearest vision for our purpose in life.

In this chapter, we're going to discuss the importance of having the right people around us, the types of individuals to avoid, and how to develop strong relationships.

We all know that for power to flow through an electrical current, there must be connection. But too often, once we've been hurt, our subconscious belief systems regarding self-preservation will cause us to pull away from people, stop trusting, and attempt going through life on our own. This knee-jerk reaction can cause us to abandon the very support group that we will need to weather the more challenging conditions that will come as we move along the journey of life.

I believe the deepest-rooted belief system we must face and overcome daily is the one called "self-preservation." Thankfully, this self-preservation programming exists to keep us alive, to keep us from overlooking danger, and to enable us to respond to scenarios that could possibly harm us. However, since we now live in a world that is relatively safe from natural threats like the ones humans faced thousands of years ago, this need to look out for ourselves is often expressed through the over-inflation of otherwise nonthreatening details from our daily lives. For example, we often unnecessarily feel anxious or paranoid that others may be speaking negatively about us, planning to take something of importance from us (like a position or a promotion), or even planning to do us physical harm. As a result, we develop unconscious prejudices against other people and retreat to a mental island of isolation, making true-life advancement much more difficult.

Patrick Lencioni says, "Teamwork begins with the building of trust, and the only way to do that is to overcome our need for invulnerability." Our fears of being vulnerable stem from this self-preservation lens that we wear all the time. As a person of faith, I believe that we must face the fear of abandonment, embarrassment, and vulnerability by embracing the qualities of boldness and courage that exemplify the LION leader. When we allow the fears of being hurt, embarrassed, or even abandoned to override our awareness that we need a strong team around us, we drift off into solitude, making molehills into mountains, and missing out on the creative energy that can be harnessed when we collaborate with a team. It was Helen Keller who first said, "Alone we can do so little, but together we can do so much." Likewise, Louisa May Alcott said, "It takes two flints to make a fire."

Over the past decade, I can reflect on the years when I was on the road, by myself, trying to create success. The long plane rides, hotel stays, and taxicab trips began to take a toll on me in many different ways. I remember the times where the work itself replaced my spiritual practice, the very thing that had once given me so much joy, peace, and vitality. Being caught in the routine of pushing, grinding, and working by myself as I tried to make the world a better place almost got the best of me. Then, six years ago, my mentor Mr. Klemmer suddenly passed away. I came to the realization that I would soon have to step away from his company and begin to build my own company and brand. It was at that time that I experienced even more solitude than I had before. Since I wasn't traveling as often, I was spending much of my time, alone in my office, trying to drum up speaking opportunities and create new content for resources to sell. It was during these times that I eventually came face-to-face with my deepest-rooted fears. Money was tight, stress was high, and I felt like I had no one that could help me to navigate the sea that I often felt I was sinking into.

However, by continuing to visualize the end result that I desired, keeping myself focused by reading and studying new materials, and even creating new materials of my own, good things slowly began to happen. I'm so grateful for the love and support of my wife Jennifer during those tough times. Without her, I don't know how I would have made it all happen. Our team, though it was small at the time, was committed to never quitting. We worked hard and sowed seeds that eventually began to produce fruit. Slowly we stopped treading water and began to make some real progress toward our goals. We met the right people and worked hard to serve those relationships in the best way we knew how. These connections then paved the way for us to be able to pay the bills and also pour some extra money into the next level. I can say now that through our company's monthly video membership program, speaking engagements, audio resources and coaching clients, we are doing very well! But, I want to emphasize that our success is only made possible because of our connections, the connection that Jennifer and I have with each other and the connections that we've made with others along the way. Making the right connections, by being AVAILABLE as well as PREPARED, definitely opened many great doors for us.

Below are five reasons why CONNECTIONS are so important.

1. Connections give us much-needed encouragement.

Alexander Graham Bell said, "When one door closes, another one opens." We often look so long and so regretfully upon the closed door that we do not see the ones that have opened. The right connections can keep us looking toward what we do have and what we can achieve, rather than what we don't have. Ultimately, the right connections offer us a source of hope and inspiration. You see, there's nothing more exciting than spending time with people that have a vision for their life and are so excited about their vision that it inspires you to expand your own.

One of the great connections that I have is my dear friend, Danny Chambers. Danny and I have been friends for over six years. His words of encouragement always speak life into me and help me to think bigger, stay the course, and believe for the next level. This divine connection is one that I believe God has orchestrated to help both of us as we move into the next seasons of our lives. Because Danny has succeeded on so many levels, he knows how to help me avoid potential blind spots. His wisdom aids me in shortening some of the learning curves I encounter as I work to expand my reach in the world. On top of that, Danny is also a terrific husband to his wife Jillian and father to their 5 children. Both Danny and Jillian are great examples of leadership, encouragement and compassion. Having great encouragers in your life will help you to find the strength necessary as you navigate the tough times and push to the next level.

2. Connections give you a place to share your fears, worries, and concerns.

"No man is an island unto himself." We are all connected in some way, and we get better and stronger when we have those around us that can help lighten our load. Sometimes the greatest thing we can do for someone who is experiencing the pain of a defeat or loss is to simply offer our time and be there for them in whatever capacity they may need. In the workshops that I have done around the world I've learned that many people who are experiencing pain or loss believe that they are the only ones who have ever experienced that pain. Their feelings of solitude and loneliness actually compound the effects of pain and can cause a person to "self-destruct" emotionally as they believe that they have no one to turn to. We often create these thoughts unconsciously because being vulnerable and asking for help could potentially lead to someone else hurting us even more deeply. If we can learn to assist in carrying the burdens of others when they are struggling, we become stronger to handle our own, and we eventually reap the rewards from the seeds of compassion that we have sown. The English novelist and philosopher Aldous Huxley said, "Experience is not what happens to you, it is what you do with what happens to you." We are all going to experience the pains of loss, death, sickness and defeat at some time in our lives, but having a support team around us can help to lighten the load and remain hopeful. And, as Aldous Huxley implied, do something positive with the experiences.

3. Connections provide valuable feedback.

At NASA there are currently three main divisions working together on the upcoming Mars Mission. The first group, GSDO, or Ground Systems Development and Operations, is based at Kennedy Space Center and deals with the systems on the ground that will keep the spacecraft operational. The second division is Space Launch Systems, otherwise known as SLS. This is the division that represents the rockets and teams that will work together to create a means for astronauts to travel far into deep space. The third division is known as Orion. This division comprises of the actual capsule that will launch from the top of the SLS. The Orion spacecraft is intended to carry a crew of four astronauts to the desired destination in outer space.

Each of these divisions plays a major role in the success of the mission. Can you imagine a spacecraft with four well-trained astronauts shooting into outer space, only to have no communications with the ground to help them navigate their voyage? We've already discussed the miraculous return of Apollo 13, the mission that encountered a nearly fatal explosion while in outer space that could have destroyed the spacecraft and killed the astronauts on board. We learned that with the teamwork, commitment and collaboration of all parties involved, the spacecraft and the astronauts were able to return safely back to Earth. The phrase "failure is not an option" was coined during the Apollo 13 mission, and it is one I believe we can all apply to our personal life missions.

Have you ever considered that your life is a mission that it is unfolding every day? And have you considered just how important your mission is? Have you thought of the people who will follow you in generations to come, and the impact that your mission will have on them? If so, I think it is important for us to also realize that this mission will require many people along the way to make it successful. Not only those who can cheer for us during the good times, but also those who can help us to navigate when things are not so good. Feedback from these people will help us to see what we otherwise might not have seen and avoid accidents that could cost us time and money. Great teams use feedback as the vitamins to help keep them healthy and functioning well.

4. Connections give us strength in areas where we are weak.

All strong leaders that I know and have the opportunity to work with, have strong teams with a diversity of gifts and talents. Even celebrities that we see on the cover of magazines, TV and film have a team of people - a manager, dietician, attorney, personal trainer, etc. - to keep them healthy and in their lane moving forward. Nothing is more frustrating than having a specific gift that you're not utilizing often enough because you have to do menial tasks that could easily be done by someone else.

For example, if your gifts are not financial management and accounting, you should quickly find someone who is not only good at financial management but that is also passionate about it. It is also important that they have your best interest at heart. Many individuals, including myself in the past, have gotten behind in financial matters because of a lack of knowledge and accountability that can help us to stay current and ahead of the game.

Having the right connections will keep you from wasting valuable time that could be used to propel you forward. Every astronaut, when working on a mission, has a team of individuals monitoring their heart rate and breathing. Often when an astronaut is focused on a particular task in outer space, he or she has the potential to get worked up. When this happens, it creates more of a chance that they could get hurt in the formidable conditions of outer space.

Having a support team on the ground allows the astronaut to do what he or she needs to do while having someone in their corner looking out for them. This is true of all teamwork. Author Simon Sinek says, "Passion is about working hard doing what you love, but stress is about working hard doing things you care nothing about." Each of us has a passion inside that can truly carry us to places that many people will never get to go to. But, we must understand that we can't do it alone! The journey of success is too long and too challenging to think that we can do it without the support of others.

In the early 1970s, Bill Gates and his business partner, Paul Allen, started a company that created no real success. Years later, Allen said that they failed so miserably with that first company, Traf-o-data, they had no choice but to begin to work diligently on what would eventually become Microsoft. If you consider that the wealthiest man in the world started his first company which failed "miserably," you can stop beating yourself up for the times that you might have mis-planned, mis-performed and fallen short. As I have said so many times before, "failure is not the opposite of success, it is simply a part of it." As Gates and Allen have shown, that early endeavor led them to begin developing the new products that have granted them status as some of the most successful and influential people in the world.

I want to take a moment to remind you that Bill Gates' story is not just about his financial success; it's also important to remember that his technological innovations have completely transformed the computer industry. Much of what you can do on a computer now is a direct result of the work that Gates and Allen have done.

Too often, we take a temporary setback and make it a permanent failure because we don't have someone around to help us to get back up when we've been knocked off course. Even the greatest fighters in the world - Mike Tyson, Muhammad Ali, and even George Foreman - all had a coach in their corner, helping them to study their opponent, stay focused, and never quit. Bob Bowman, swimming trainer of Michael Phelps, helped to train and mentor Phelps on his journey to become the most decorated Olympic athlete of all time. Bowman has said that Phelps swam 365 days a year for six years in a row, and he only knew that because he was there each day, watching him and helping him improve.

So how does an athlete like Michael Phelps become the most decorated Olympian of all time? Practice. And, what drives a person to practice that much? The answer is, passion and accountability. By having someone on our team who can help us to begin again each day, no matter what obstacles we may have faced the day before, we begin to maximize the time that many others forfeit because they lack the motivation and accountability to begin again. This is not to say that we must rely solely on someone else to motivate us, but we sure do need someone to help us push through on the days that we're struggling to find the drive. As we *"act our way into feeling,"* we become more productive than if we were to *"feel our way into acting."* Having someone push us into action can help us find the feelings necessary to carry on. Feelings are far too unreliable to be counted on, so having this person in our corner that can help to strengthen us where and when we are weak, is extremely valuable.

5. Connections give us a mirror to see how we are growing and where we need to improve.

It is easy to **seem** enlightened, mature, and at peace when you live secluded "in a cave" and don't have to deal with people on a day-to-day basis. As we navigate through life - dealing with people's personalities, programming, and problems - we get to see exactly where we stand and how much we still have to mature. Once we mature past the early stages of not wanting to "share our toys at playtime," we begin to see that, in order to be successful, we must not fight to win battles that are not worthy of our time. In short, we must learn to develop strong allies, not strong enemies. The strength of our connections will reveal how well we are doing in the area of growth and maturity.

Now that we've discussed the importance of connections, I want to share some qualities that you should definitely look for in those you wish to connect with. Not to mention some qualities you should definitely avoid. No matter how hard we try, we will encounter people that we will later wish we had never met. It is often in those heartaches and letdowns that we discover something valuable about ourselves. I have heard it said, "temporary people can teach us permanent lessons."

Here are a few of my own personal rules regarding how I associate with others.

Rule #1: Never share your problems with people who don't have the capacity to help you solve them.

I call it "putting your business on the street." Let's face

it - we all have things that we might not be so proud of. But, we do not need to give anyone any information that they might exaggerate, misunderstand, or use to negatively impact how others may see us.

Rule #2: Do not associate with people who are willing to waste your time.

If someone is not considerate enough to be on time for a meeting with you, he or she does not fully value who you are. In time, that dishonor will show itself in other ways. I am careful with my money and I am equally careful with my time.

Rule #3: Refrain from going into business with anyone who speaks negatively about his or her spouse.

When a person speaks negatively about their spouse, it's not a spouse issue, it's a heart issue. Eventually, the heart issue they have with their spouse will be directed toward you when you make a mistake. I'm not saying this to pass judgment on anyone who may be having marital problems, those things happen. However, what I am saying is be cautious of people that speak negatively about others, especially the people that they are closest to. If they will talk negatively about them, they will speak negatively about you.

Rule #4: Never begin a partnership or business relationship with someone who has a substance abuse problem.

Struggling with substance abuse doesn't make someone a person bad but from a business relationship standpoint, it simply adds too many variables to the success equation. Creating success that is impactful and long lasting is tough enough as it is, we don't need to add more challenges. I doubt that NASA would trust one of their spacecraft to someone who was struggling to get control of drugs or alcohol. If you need to, get the person the help he or she needs, but do not try to rescue them with all your time and energy - especially when you are trying to get your own business off the ground. It may feel good to try and help all the time, but in the end, the individual must be willing to help him or herself. I have seen too many people that have lost years of their life trying to rescue someone from a place that they really didn't want to be rescued from. Not in all cases, but in many cases, people just like to stay stuck and get attention from others with their "victim" mindset.

Rule #5: Avoid developing relationships with people who appear needy.

When a person doesn't have a proper relationship with him or herself, they will look to you to fulfill those psychological and emotional needs. These types of relationships are sure to cause much emotional stress between you and the other person. No one is going to be perfect, but it's best to try and work with people that are confident in who they are and not looking to you to provide their sense of well-being. We can often tend to feel guilty when we don't give ourselves to someone that appears "needy" but in the end you will move forward much faster than you would "fixing" someone else's emotional issues.

Rule #6: Refrain from getting too close to anyone who enjoys stirring up gossip.

There's an old saying: "If they will talk about other people, they will talk about you." Many people have nothing better to do than speak negatively about those who are trying to do something positive with their life. Gossip is a deal killer for me when it comes to building a team.

Rule #7: Keep yourself from developing deep relationships with those who have no goals.

Over the years I have seen that people who do not have a goal to work toward, easily get stuck in unproductive behaviors and habits. Working with people that have no goals or direction can lead to frustration, or worse, you may even begin to exhibit some of their unproductive attitudes and behaviors. If you want to soar like an eagle, you can't hang around with chickens. I know that we are all created equally but our habits and disciplines are what set us apart in the marketplace. Work with people that will help you to pull away from the crowds of complacency.

****

I want to close this chapter with an idea. As you start to develop a team that can help you all to achieve the success you desire, you need to understand that having "attractive" people in your life means you must continually work to make yourself more "attractive." Obviously I'm **not** talking about superficial attractive qualities. Yes, I do believe that it's important for us to work on our outward appearance, as the world we live in does notice - and is quite judgmental of

- our appearance. But, the attractiveness I'm talking about is more of a being-ness that one possesses, aside from how he or she simply appears on the outside. Think about this: How would you appear to a person who has no eyesight? Would you appear to be kind, sensitive, compassionate, intelligent and capable? Or would you appear negative, unconcerned, casual, closed-minded or immature?

Many people spend so much of their resources trying to put things on the outside of their body that they don't have many resources left to invest on their mind. Unfortunately, the concept of self-improvement and personal development has not yet "dawned" on everyone. Many people are simply inching toward old age without truly being intentional about their own personal growth. So often we see people who only want to talk about how things used to be instead of talking about what could be. As a good friend of mine always says, "Getting old is easy, but getting better takes work."

I once had a 90-plus-year-old lady in a seminar that I was facilitating. She was just as excited to learn as anyone else! She was also quick to share that she believed that when she stopped learning, she would begin dying. And it was clear that she didn't want that to happen!

As we raise our children, I don't believe that we should

raise them to **have** more than we have. I believe, instead that we should raise them to **become** more than we are. If we develop them into strong leaders, the "having more" part will more than likely take care of itself. There's a wonderful poem that reads:

"A careful man I want to be; a little fellow follows me

I do not dare to go astray, for fear that he will go the self-same way I cannot once escape his eyes; whatever he sees me do, he tries

Like me he says he's going to be, that little chap who follows me

He thinks I am so very fine, believes in every word of mine

The base in me he must not see, the little chap who follows me

I must remember as I go, through summer's sun and winter's snow

I'm building for the years to be, the little chap who follows me."

This poem speaks so loudly regarding the importance of doing what is right for the sake of those who may be watching. We can often become blind to our own behaviors, but those who look up to us - our children, neighbors, team members, family, etc. - are very impacted by what we do. Film producer Gale Ann Hurd said, "If you can't find a good role model, simply be one." As we look for the right relationships to develop with others, we always have a terrific opportunity to work on the most important relationship of all, the one we have with our self.

Before moving on to the next chapter, I encourage you to take time to reflect on the relationships that you have. What are the qualities you admire in those people and how could you develop those qualities in your own personal life. Winning teams have winning people, and in order to win, we must be willing to be our best.

CHAPTER 10

Take Action

"Adversity introduces a man to himself."

Albert Einstein

So far, we've already discussed numerous topics. We have discussed changing old belief systems, developing a healthy perspective of our past, having a forward-thinking mindset, and how to develop the relationships that will take us to the next level. In this chapter, we are going to discuss taking action on our goals and what it takes to maintain momentum.

It truly is the small adjustments that we make on a daily basis that make the biggest difference when it comes to our long-term success. Since this is the only life we get, it's very important to do the small things daily that can make our lives richer, more rewarding and more enjoyable. If you want to change your life, you must be willing to change at least one thing that you do each day. There's power in simplicity and consistency, and there's no need to overwhelm yourself by trying to change dozens of things at once. Just be willing to get started, make necessary adjustments and keep moving. Over time you will produce stronger, more fulfilling results.

In order to take action, or change the actions we're already taking, I believe we must first address our attitudes. Oprah Winfrey said, "The greatest discovery of all time is that a person can change their life simply by changing their attitude," and the most important attitude that we possess is the attitude about who we believe we are. I believe that when we begin to develop a different attitude regarding our identity and our future potential, we will naturally begin taking the necessary steps that will lead us to a more compelling life.

Mistaken Identities

If I were to ask you, "Who are you?" you would probably tell me your profession, or tell me that you're a mother or father, wife or husband, sister or brother. The problem with these types of answers is that, when you so quickly align with a "label" that doesn't fully identify who you are, you end up limiting the perspective you have of yourself.

If a person is labeled "doctor," your mind may naturally begin to assign all sorts of attributes to that person, many of which could be false. You may know nothing about their life, family, hurts, joys or interests. The person to you is simply "doctor."

This type of thinking has been engrained into us by a culture and society that causes us to overlook the true depth of other human beings. Over time, we can begin to do the same thing with ourselves. Once a person has worked to obtain a title, they often will work the rest of their life to uphold the image that they believe comes with that title. This is one of the reasons why titles can be so dangerous to true self-expression.

It has been said that we are the sum total of the choices that we've made in the past. I do agree with this to some degree. Without memory of our past we could lose some of the wisdom that comes from our experiences. However, I also believe that your life is simply what you choose to create on a moment-to-moment basis *currently*. As the rapper DMX once said in his lyrics, "This is life." What he meant was, this is it, right now. There is nothing else. As we all know, a person can be alive for many years yet be so mentally "busy" that he or she never really lives. Life, to many, is simply a blur; and when we don't take the time to slow down to get focused and create the life we want, we live a life of default. Often our "default" mode is based on our reactions to what has already been done in our past. In other words, our present is often just a reflection of our interpretations of past events.

The good news is that every moment holds within it the power to shift out of what was once "normal" into something completely new. Most of us miss these opportunities, however, because we assume that our only options are the ones that we have considered previously. Even as you read this, you are filtering this information through old programming. It can be difficult to establish new ways of thinking, especially if we have been thinking a certain way for long periods of time.

We typically reject new possibilities and instead focus on what we are used to seeing. Or, at least what we *expect* to see. We also have a way of disregarding many of the things that we don't expect to see and instead focus in on the things that we can more easily comprehend because of familiarity. This can also cause us to label people and situations, putting them into a "category" that we feel most comfortable with. We then look to reinforce again and again the initial labeling that we've done. This is what psychologists refer to as

"Confirmation Bias." This is why we hear sayings like, "You only have one chance to make a first impression." Once we see someone a certain way, we attach a label through which we will likely always filter our interactions and impressions of them. We notice things that REAFFIRM our beliefs more often and tend to overlook things that could change our thinking about them.

So, the question I posed earlier was actually a bit of a trick question. When I asked you who you are, your response was probably just the label that you have placed on yourself. Now, if I were to ask you to rate yourself on a scale of 1 to 10 in the areas of beauty, intelligence, passion, discipline, and courage, how would you answer? And how would you determine what a '1' represents versus a '10'?

You may not realize it, but you have created your own measure of "reality" based on the labels you have put on yourself and others. The scale you have in your mind is constructed by what you choose to believe. There is no true, universal scale when it comes to your opinions; you're simply making it all up as you go. So, since you're creating the scale, why not create a scale that causes you to feel really good about yourself and confident enough to take massive action toward your dreams?

No matter what you are facing, whether you're waiting until you move into your dream home or until you reach a certain body type, the reality is that your experience is your OWN creation. No one can design your life or create your experience for you. This is your journey and you are writing the script every single day. When you think in a way that supports your overall well-being and happiness, you will get exited about holding the pen, and you'll get even more serious about who you allow to write on your life's paper.

The teams that we're a part of needs us to be our best so that we can help others team members become their best. Whether you want to admit it or not, the old saying is true: "A chain is only as strong as it's weakest link." Our friends, our families and the people we work with most closely will have a much better experience with us when we become intentional about the experience we are creating for ourselves. If we aren't creating a positive experience, it is hard to share a positive experience with anyone else. The source of energy that you choose to tap into will inevitably be the energy that you share. So, if we really do care about our family, friends and teams, shouldn't we get really serious about the quality of the experience that we share with them? You will either be a thermometer that reads the temperature, or you will be a thermostat that changes the temperature. You really are that powerful!

All great teams need people who are willing to step up their own game and share their energy with others. Don't wait for someone else to do it; you do it! And always try to remember what Winston Churchill said: "Attitude is the little thing that can make a huge difference." Never let what anyone else may say about you to determine the image that you have of yourself. Your overall attitude is said to simply be your stored, emotional history. To have a stronger identity and better attitude, focus on the things that have worked for you in your life and keep your focus off of the things that stir up negative emotions.

Attitude Shifts and Action Steps

Maintaining a positive attitude that inspires action isn't always easy. The good news is that the more you practice it, the easier it gets. Like learning to cook or learning to paint, you must practice at your positive attitude daily and eventually it will become more second nature. I believe that what you do daily, you become permanently. If you want to get better at experiencing more joy and happiness in your life, you must be willing to practice.

If you can start to do enough things on the outside that trigger a positive response from you on the inside, you will gain more control of your thinking and your feelings. You've heard me say that atmosphere often determines how we feel. As a leader, you must be willing to put yourself into atmospheres that demand the best version of yourself. If you do not like to get out and socialize, but know it would help you in your business, career, or personal life, you must be willing to "put yourself out there." If you don't like to exercise but you know you want to lose weight, you have to be willing to set some sort of fitness goal and then get some accountability that will help you to take action.

You will be amazed at what happens to your thinking when you begin to put yourself in situations that you normally wouldn't put yourself into. In this case, positive action leads to the attitude shifts that will inspire even more positive action. If you don't make time, you'll never find time, and there is so much more to life than sitting around waiting on your emotions to lead you. LION leaders never wait on their emotions to take some action, **we lead our emotions by taking the action.** Emotions are far too unreliable to count on when we are serious about creating true success. Emotions can tend to change depending on what time of month it is, what day of the week it is, what you've eaten, the weather outside, and how everyone else is behaving.

When I took control of my life, it came in direct proportion to my willingness to design my daily activities with intention. I stopped planning things based on how I felt. Average people wait to see how the day will go; leaders design their day and then attack it. You are either fighting for a compelling life or you're settling for a mediocre one.

How will you start taking the action that will ultimately change the course of your life? Are you going to keep talking about what you're going to do or are you going to take some steps now that will lead you in the right direction? Make more moves and make less announcements!

Here are some pointers:

Start small.

Determine one single activity that you could add to your week that will make your life more fulfilling and will eventually move you closer toward your desired life.

Write it down on a sheet of paper and hang it somewhere that you will notice.

Your bedroom or your bathroom is a perfect spot. Each time you walk past the paper, you'll see that there is something more that you can do to help you achieve your goals. This will keep it on your mind as a focal point, and you'll be more likely to actually do it.

Follow through and then write out your next goal.

I do this often with a whiteboard in my office that hangs beside the door. As I go in and out of my office I always see what goal I have written there. It can almost become annoying to keep seeing the same thing over and over again, if I haven't taken any action toward accomplishing it. This frustration can be the precipitator that pushes me to take action.

This strategy of putting your goals up on a board can work for any area of life that you would like to focus on. If you take time to write it on the outside, it can provoke something within you on the inside.

If you don't create some external stimuli, you may stay in the same mode for weeks, months, or even years and never achieve even the smallest goals. This is the pattern of life that so many fall into! Remember, to succeed we must first believe that we can. By writing something down, we are making a declaration that it **IS** possible.

Eventually you'll find yourself going from a single sheet of paper by the door to post-it notes all over your home, all over your office, and even in your car. It really does work! You'd be amazed at how much time you can find for things when you intentionally plan them out. Conversely, if you're not willing to do even these small things to make your goals happen, you shouldn't expect to achieve them.

It's these small reminders that will help you to keep your mind open to new possibilities. As I mentioned earlier, I wake up early to get my daily workout in before I do anything else. But, I wasn't always a morning person! I decided to make some changes to my schedule by signing up and paying for early morning workout classes. By making myself accountable I began to do something that rewired my thinking. I now know that the more we see ourselves in action, the more we believe that specific action is a part of who we are. By writing your goals and keeping them in a visible place, you will be reminded of what action you need to take, even when the busyness of life can cause you to forget.

This is a great time to share what the word "ACTION" means to me.

A stands for Align

It is so important for you to align with a purpose and goal that is will require a better version of yourself. I've always said, "The stages of life are Learn, Earn and Return." When we're aligned with a bigger purpose in life, we're more willing to return some of the resources that we've gained to make a bigger difference in the world.

C stands for Commit

You may *want* to produce great results, but if you're not *committed* to consistently doing the small things well along the way, you will never produce them. The difference between a "want" and a "commitment" are as different as a lightening bug and lightening. We must get committed to the things that we want to produce, by doing small things well on a daily basis that will lead us to achievement. Saying you want to make the world a better place is not enough!

T stands for Transition

We discussed navigating transitions in an earlier chapter and how, if we're going to transition effectively, we will have to move past some of our old mindsets and beliefs. One of the challenges with transition is that, during this time, you're in "no-man's land." That is, you haven't yet achieved what you want, but you've let go of something that you once held to in the past. This feeling of transition can often be an uneasy one, but as we navigate the transitions, we become stronger; increase capacity and develop perspectives that will help maintain success. The transitions are where we find our strength and develop the patience that will carry us through to the next level.

I stands for Impart

Speaking life into your situation and imparting words of wisdom, knowledge, and positivity are so vitally important. Many times people overlook the importance of their words and they start speaking negatively along the way. I've often said that if you litter your days with negativity, don't be surprised when you look up one day and you have a trashy life. To lead ourselves and lead others well, we must learn to use our words as weapons to defeat fear, doubt and negativity. We may never get rid of the negative voices in our head but we can surely dilute it with positive words. You hear every word you say, both internally and externally, so make sure that you are speaking in a way that compels you to move forward. We must learn to talk to ourselves, not listen to ourselves. When I got control of my words, I got control of my world.

O stands for Observe

Through observation, you should be continually making honest assessments of your results - and being willing to make the necessary adjustments along the way. Many people have what I call the "Arrow mentality." The arrow mentality is where, once we begin heading toward our target, we don't make any adjustment if the target were to move. I believe success is definitely a moving target and we must be willing to adjust. Instead of being like an "arrow," think of yourself more as a "heat-seeking missile." A heat-seeking missile makes adjustments every moment to make sure it winds up hitting the target even as the target continues to move. As we strive to gain momentum with our actions, it's very important for us to look at what we're doing on a day-to-day basis, and make the tweaks that will help us to arrive at our desired destination. Don't get stuck by turning a "blind eye" to the adjustments that need to be made consistently on the road to success. Look for obstacles and make the adjustments.

N stands for Never quit

Never give yourself the option to quit! When you refuse to give yourself the option to quit you'll be forced to continue to do the right things when before you might have quit. Doing the right things, even when we don't feel like it, leads to gaining momentum, and in the end, produces success.

Action dissolves fear. So many people operate with fear in their life because they've never faced their fears. When we do the things that are difficult, we gain more confidence and an enhanced self-image. Once we begin to feel better about ourselves, we will feel more inclined to tackle even tougher challenges. With my career, I never gave myself a "Plan B." I was only concerned with finding ways to make my "Plan A" work better. The acceptance of challenges, and the growth that comes with them, is exactly how LION leaders are developed. You truly are much more capable than you probably give yourself credit for.

Friction As Fertilizer

Leaders are not born; they are developed! They are chiseled out of the rock called "average" and polished by the friction of life's tougher issues. If you get offended and frustrated with every single rub, how will you ever expect to be polished? You've got to use each day to gain momentum, stay focused, and see what it is that you can become. William Arthur Ward said, "Adversity causes some men to break, and other men to break records." And it was Albert Einstein who said, "Adversity introduces a man to himself."

With all of this in mind, I encourage you to create some adversity or challenging situations, as they are ultimately the fertilizer that will help you grow into the LION leader you were destined to be. Now, I do not mean that you should create drama or devastation for yourself or your family through bad choices.

I simply mean pushing yourself and immersing yourself in the situations that require you to grow into a stronger, better person. By doing this, you will start to see how much you can handle. If you ever want to be able to bench-press 250 pounds, you're going to have to start out with much less weight and work your way up. This principle works the same way with our mind and our emotions. As we get stronger and stronger, the weight or issue that once seemed huge, is no longer as difficult to handle.

When challenges come, it's our point of focus that actually drives how we feel. But, by developing momentum - by putting notes and reminders around your home, in your office, and in your car - you will be reminded to stay focused on where you're headed, and not just the challenge that is at hand. Just because a storm is going on around us, doesn't mean that the storm has to go on within you.

Dale Carnegie said, "We must learn to develop success from our failures. Discouragement and failure are two of the surest stepping stones to success." If you won't push yourself and be willing to fail, you'll never change the limiting story and the labels that you have created for yourself. Frank Clark said, "If you can find a path with no obstacles, it is sure not to lead anywhere."

Of everything that I have shared with you in this book so far, I want you to know that this truth resonates with me the most: You are a powerful being, and the only thing that can stop you from achieving anything you desire is simply an unwillingness to push yourself, and fail to develop the necessary disciplines. By failing and choosing to get up again, you send a very valuable message to yourself. When you push yourself just a little bit harder than you have in your past, you send a valuable message to yourself. When you consistently do what is hard versus what is easy, you send a valuable message to yourself. Once you begin to recognize that maybe you were wrong about all the limiting labels and stories that you have told yourself over the years, you will become unstoppable.

A powerful question to ask yourself each day when you wake up is, "What will I create today?" Not, "What will I react to today?," or "How will I label things today?," but "What will I create?" Your past is powerless until you recall it. Your yesterday is weak compared to the strength of the present moment, and the potential of now far outweighs the possibilities of the time that has passed. So embrace this moment! Break free of the bondage from your past interpretations, and turn the page of old to begin to write about what can be. A scripture from the New Testament of the bible reads, "Do not conform to this world, but be transformed by the renewing of your mind." Do you know that your identity, how you see yourself and how you feel about yourself, is all stored in your mind? Your mind is the control center for your life. If you don't learn to take control of it, it will always have control of you.

When we reassess situations and choose to look at them in a renewed way, we become powerful. This renewal is simply an act of creation. As my mentor used to say, "To think is to create." Going back to an original state of mind means that we're open to a fresh perspective.

Albert Einstein said, "We cannot solve a problem by using the same thinking that we created it with." Since our past is already done, and it cannot be changed, the only way to have a new experience of it is to simply change our perspective. When we change the way we look at things, the things we look at change.

I challenge you to think back on a hurtful relationship or event in the past, and then renew your mind by creating a new story regarding it. Begin to look at the positive lessons that you learned, and look for the blessings that you received. Once you begin to do this, you are ready to begin healing. Until then, you'll continue to carry the same old perspectives, and the same old labels, which lead to the same old pain.

Your renewed perspective may not change the person who hurt you, but it will free you from having to carry the same old emotions that they contributed to. Remember, it is feelings that typically drive our actions, and if we want to act better, it's up to us to start feeling better. The only benefit of carrying pain from the past is that we get to be RIGHT about it. We get to KEEP our initial perspectives and tell ourselves how intelligent we are. We also get to tell ourselves how "wrong" everyone else is. The concept of certainty can lead us down a road of unhappiness and frustration! Renewing our mind is a powerful way to stay present and start to enjoy our life even more. What if you took a painful event from your past and tried to look at the situation for the perspective of the person who hurt you? What could they have been feeling or going through at the time of the event? We are all dealing with challenges that many other people know nothing about. When we respect this, we realize that none of us are perfect. From this place, we are better able to offer the grace and forgiveness that we would hope to receive if we had made a similar mistake.

A renewed mind gives us our power back. We can then direct that power into the actions that will help us to make a better difference in this world. People do awful things, but if we're unwilling to renew our minds, the thing that has already been done will hurt us again and again. If we keep RE-calling an event it doesn't have to RE-occur to keep hurting us. You don't have to forget what happened, but you can surely forget the old label that you placed on it. Choose to create a new label that serves you. Do this with your job. Do this in your marriage, with your family and with yourself.

LION leaders carry the scars, but release the pain. We take the lessons, and leave the guilt. You will never lead others well if you're unwilling to lead yourself. You deserve better, and you're worthy of more! Take the ACTION to master your mind and you will move forward, faster than you ever have before. Always remember the words of Zig Ziglar, "If something is worth doing, it is worth doing wrong until you get it right." Keep taking action and soon you will see that there truly are no limits to what is possible.

CHAPTER 11

Lead Like a LION

"*Your biggest opportunity may be right here,
where you are, right now.*"

Napoleon Hill

After doing hundreds of leadership training events around the world, and speaking to tens of thousands of people, I truly believe that the biggest challenge we have as leaders is our unwillingness to let go of the image of the person we used to be. We have become so accustomed to the familiar that we unconsciously resist the very change that is trying to be expressed through us. I have recently adopted a new quote that says, "I'm not who I used to be, and I'm not who I'm going to be." When we think in this way, we are inclined to focus not on how things once appeared but on how we can use what we have available to us that can help us create a better tomorrow.

I'm reminded of a quote by Napoleon Hill: "Your

biggest opportunity may be right here, where you are, right now." Likewise, General George S. Patton said, "A good plan violently executed right now is better than a perfect plan executed next week."

We must make the firm commitment each day to take full advantage of the moment at hand. We must not develop patterns of waiting on better conditions, because the truth is, they may not. Instead, we need to take every moment to do the work necessary to reach our fullest potential.

With that in mind, below are seven specific qualities that I believe are required of us if we are truly going to become LION leaders and be able to lead others the way we were meant to lead.

Self-Awareness

The quality of self-awareness is paramount when it comes to taking control of our thinking, feelings, desires and impulses. As a dear friend of mine always says, "What you don't take hold of now will soon take hold of you." So when we choose to hold onto a preconceived notion of who we think we are instead of having the courage to open our minds and consider what's possible, we begin to repeat the same activities again and again. Those activities then lead to the same results, and those results affirm our initial notions of who it is that we think we are.

We've talked about this repeatedly throughout the book, but this concept is important enough to repeat. The shift into LION leadership begins when we admit that, in order for new patterns to emerge, old patterns must die. Our ego will create lies, distractions, false scenarios, and even imaginary limitations to keep us on the defensive. We must be aware of this and remain on the offensive as opposed to the defensive.

I don't believe that we get to arrive at the next level simply because we've gotten bored with this one. Breaking through to the next level in life - whether it's in relationships, finances, physical health, or even career - will require an unrelenting courage and boldness that few people will muster. Many people claim to know that there's no excuse for mediocrity but they will spend much of their life looking for one. In fact, I truly believe that one of the only reasons we're not already at the next level that we seek is because of a lack of the disciplines that are required to get us there.

If we were to choose each day to move past our fear of failure and get absolutely committed to producing results no matter what the cost, we would make huge strides toward our desired outcomes.

Back in September of 2015, I went to Kennedy Space Center at Cape Canaveral, Florida to do my first one-day training with members of NASA's lion leadership program. For the months leading up to the training I prepared and then prepared some more. I used my feelings of uncertainty and nervousness to compel me to do the things that would be necessary for me to perform well when the opportunity arrived.

Too often we can allow anxiety and frustration to shut us down! But, I believe that by keeping the right perspective, we can actually use that energy to spring us into action. That's exactly what I did for the months, weeks and days leading up to my first NASA event.

I remember driving from Orlando over to the space center on a dreary, overcast day looking out across the water to get my first glimpse of the Vehicle Assembly Building from miles away. In all honesty, I felt intimidated. The VAB is the fourth-largest building in the world and is said to be able to house over 100 Costco buildings. The American flag that hangs on the front of the VAB is 22 stories tall and the stripes on the flag are as wide as a Greyhound Bus.

Driving toward my hotel that day, it was as if the building were calling out to me, trying to provoke feelings of fear and failure. As I became aware of the negative thoughts that were attempting to infiltrate my mind, I began to think of all the hours of preparation that I had put in, the disciplines that I had developed, and the qualities that I was committed to demonstrating during my time there. As a result, the next day, at the end of the nine-hour session, one of the coordinators of the training said, "Ronnie, you're one of the best breaths of fresh air that we've ever seen. Thank you for what you did here today." I responded with "thank you very much" on the outside but was bursting with excitement on the inside. As I began to reflect on the hours of preparation that I had done, I was reminded that anything is truly possible if we're willing to put in the effor. Self-awareness can enable us to fight through discouragement, frustration and the fears that may be trying to hold us back. I always say, "we must learn to talk to ourselves instead of listening to ourselves." Self-awareness is the first key to having a positive self-talk.

The day I drove off of the property at Kennedy Space Center, I began asking myself, "What's next?" I knew then that there would be another level for me, and that it was time for me to accept it. You see, awareness is the beginning of all change. We all change with age, but without the necessary self-awareness required to be live with absolute intention, it is easy to default into a life that is not our highest or best. Being a LION leader means we're willing to fight for our best! The moment we begin to believe that the next level is possible for us, we can begin to fashion the required steps to help us develop the habits we need in order to get there. I believe it's the picture of our future that we want to create that causes us to be dissatisfied with our old reality. Without awareness we can exert much of our creative energy being busy and performing activities that actually lead us AWAY from our desired goals.

Dan Brule, a pioneer in the field of "breathwork" said, "Awareness allows us to get outside of our mind and observe it in action." If we never work toward more self-awareness we can easily behave like many of the people in our society that have been programmed to spend their lives on auto-pilot, doing what others would have them to do. I believe that when you know the possibilities for your life, you're empowered, but when you decide to take ownership of possibilities, you become unstoppable. Accepting that there is change that must be made is a big step in the right direction toward success. This is what self-awareness can give us! A closed-minded fool continues to believe that his or her ways are right, even though they produce the wrong results. Awareness tells us that wrong results come from wrong actions. So, some changes must be made if we're not seeing the results we've hoped for.

Awareness also means that we understanding that the threats to our progress are both internal and external. If we don't take a break from the monotony of everyday life and take the time to rise above our programmed actions, the world will pull us into a life of regret and frustration. Whether we want to admit it or not, there is a "world system" that doesn't want us to be aware that it even exists.

This world system prevents people from seeing that "it" actually benefits from people staying sick, distracted and unfocused. If a pharmaceutical company can keep us unaware that the power that made the body also heals the body and keep us believing that our answers will always be found in a pill, it has us. Likewise, if we allow the media to distract us from focusing on doing the work to break our families out of poverty or low-income situations, we stay stuck.

Self-awareness opens our eyes to see what we can do, and what we *must* do, on a day-to-day basis to create positive change. We typically grow our successes to the level of self-awareness that we have.

If we are not aware that success can happen to us, chances are we will never achieve it. As an example, if I grew up in a town that had only two-bedroom houses, and planned to live there as an adult, I would probably build a house with two bedrooms much like the ones I had already seen. On the other hand, if someone were to take me to another town where there were bigger houses - three-, four-, and even five-bedroom houses - my awareness would immediately be expanded, and the possibility of me building a larger home would definitely increase. It works the same way with our goals.

The process of self-awareness is a continual one. When I first began to realize that awareness was a process that never ends, I became a bit discouraged. My programming caused me to want everything right away, and it told me that if I couldn't have what I wanted right away, that something must be wrong with me. Fortunately I continued to work on myself and realize that awareness is a continual process. And that process requires diligence, dedication and patience.

Here are a few questions that I believe can help you with this process of self-awareness:

- What have you decided to be right about, that has you stuck where you are?

- If you truly believed in yourself, what would you choose to do with your life?

- Who else could be negatively impacted if you choose not to give your very best?

If we want better answers in life, we must be willing to ask better questions. A LION leader has the courage to ask these tough questions and then take massive action according to their answers.

Humility

It is one thing to be aware that changes need to be made, but it is something else entirely to be humble enough to accept and implement those changes. I believe that you are either humble or in the process of being humbled. Albert Einstein said, "The more I learn, the more I realize just how much I do not know."

Nothing will hold back our growth more than believing that we already have all the answers. Confidence will get us to the door, but arrogance will get it slammed in our face. Having a PhD from "Know-It-All University" is not an accomplishment that many people will respect. In my experience over the past decade, the most powerful influencers I have ever met were the ones with the most humility. A LION doesn't have to try and convince anybody that it is a LION. It only possesses the qualities that make it a LION, and its roar simply confirms it.

It's been said that knowledge makes people humble but arrogance makes people ignorant. I also know that arrogance requires advertising, while confidence speaks for itself. There's a Chinese proverb that says, "The bigger a man's head, the bigger his headaches." We can only truly lead if there are people that are willing to follow us.

It seems that all great leaders have had a person in their life that influenced them in a positive way. I always find it interesting to see a superstar actor or athlete on the big screen and hear them talk about their grandmother or grandfather, their mother or their father, an early teacher or even a coach that gave them the confidence to pursue their dreams. In most cases, humility gave them a spirit of teachability that enabled them to achieve greatness.

With a humble spirit, a student will ask questions that require a strong answer and then he or she will be willing to go out and apply the information that has been gained. How often do we see someone hanging around an elder to get what the elder has in his or her hand, but lacks the attitude to develop what the elder has in their heart. I've heard it said that you can't teach a man a lesson that he thinks he already knows. Arrogance is simply the lock that keeps out knowledge, but humility is the key that opens the door to understanding.

Before we go any further, I would like to clear up a misconception regarding humility. I have seen many people that confuse humility with weakness. I believe that the two words have completely different meanings. When a person is truly humble, he or she knows how strong he or she can become, and he or she is willing to take the steps necessary to develop that strength. The humble person operates from a place of openness because he or she is not afraid of not already having the right answer. Meanwhile, an arrogant person fears being seen as "less than" and over compensates with a false image of "superiority."

Empathy

The third quality that I believe we must possess as a LION leader is EMPATHY. One of the great lessons I learned from my mentor, Mr. Klemmer, was this: We are all part of the human condition and we must be willing to help one another to get through it. He would go on to say, "The only thing that needs to happen for the world to go to "hell" is for a few good people to do nothing."

Webster's Dictionary defines empathy as *"a strong feeling that you understand and share another person's experiences and emotions."* Let me be clear, *it's not always about you!* When you are deeply hardwired for survival it's natural to look around to see how things might harm you. As a result, you're always unconsciously thinking about yourself. Thinking only of our self never leads to fulfillment and achievement. After all, the word "mediocrity," begins with M-E.

Relationships are the mirrors that allow us to see how we're developing on our road to personal development. The person that wants nothing to do with the team wants nothing to do with growth. Over time, this attitude of selfishness can cause us to believe that we're the center of the universe, and that everyone else is simply a prop in the play that we call *Life.* It's only when we realize that we're all created equally, and that we would do our best to respect and honor one another, that we set ourselves apart from the thinking and behaviors of so many others. It's now considered normal to be consumed with ourselves, taking selfies, and talking about ourselves constantly.

Empathy causes us to reach out a hand to those who need it. I've heard it said before that, "True empathy requires that you step outside your own emotions to view things entirely from the perspective of another person." As I have already stated, I believe that the most powerful influencers of today have a strong sense of humility. I believe that, like humility, empathy can cause us to see others in a way that is not from an elevated perspective, but of genuine concern for our fellow man. Jim Rohn once said, "Each of us is responsible for all of us, and all of us are responsible for each of us."

In today's society, with cliques, cults, tribes, clans, and clubs, it's easy to feel disconnected from those around us. The groups we find ourselves in are often the result of external appearances, lifestyle choices, personal beliefs, and political views. And it's often the process of finding those who look and think like us that causes us to judge the groups that we don't feel connected to. But judging a person does not define who they are - it defines who *we* are. When a young child grows up in a home where prejudice and judgment are taught, he or she can develop into an adult with a warped view of humanity that can ultimately result in unneeded confrontations and even indifference. I have always found it interesting how so many judge other people by the color of their skin, but we all came from the same ancestors and had no control over what color our skin would be.

When we choose to live as a LION leader, we no longer choose to hide ourselves under the rocks of ignorance and judgment. Instead, we are willing to get out of our own way and make a difference for others, regardless of their skin color, lifestyle, or beliefs. Even within the Christian faith there are more than 3600 different denominations, all believing that their theology is right. The problem is that many people have inherited their faith instead of searching for it, using their own mind and common sense. Being a Christian my whole life has given me great strength. However, I do not look down on anyone who has a different view than mine. We are all on a journey, and I think we do best when we learn to empathize with others and see things from their perspective, instead of trying to convince them that our way is right.

I believe that, too often, we filter people through one of three categories:

- People who will HELP us on our journey

- People who will HINDER us on our journey

- People who are IRRELEVANT

We must be careful to not allow our preconceived notions of others to cause us to believe that we are separate from them in any way. We will never build strong, diverse relationships and teams if we only have the capacity to work with "certain" people. I believe we should continually make assessments of our relationships to see what type of diversity we can find.

Finding out how others have been raised and how they live is an exciting thing to do! It also expands our mindset and consciousness to have greater concern for others. The Dalai Lama said, "Love is simply the absence of judgment." I believe that when we value a person enough to have a genuine concern for them, we are willing to give of ourselves generously in service to them.

As we talk about judgment, it's important to note that we must not judge ourselves too harshly, either. I love to push myself in many areas of life, but I understand the importance of giving myself the grace to make mistakes and fall short. If we make a habit of being too hard on ourselves, we aren't taking care of the vessel that God has given us to share love with others. We must love others <u>as we love ourselves</u>.

LION leaders are brave, courageous, and compassionate to everyone. Remember, it's hard to take care of others if you do not take care of yourself. The world needs you here for the long haul, so be good to you! Thus, leading others means leading yourself, taking control of yourself, and not letting your mind get the best of you.

Open-mindedness

I have a resource called *The Power of Curiosity*, and in it I discuss the challenges that come to us when we have a closed mind. Closed minds mean closed doors. If you ever want to walk through a new door, your mind needs to have already visited there.

When I share this concept with others, some people start to say things like, "Does that mean I'm supposed to be open to anything, and believe anything I hear?" The answer is absolutely NO! If you think I'm telling you to be "open-minded" when you read the newspaper, you're incorrect. I'm telling you not to read the newspaper at all! Open your mind to this idea... EVERYTHING that you're being told by the "mass media" is probably scripted by someone with an agenda.

Try instead to read new books on relationships and leadership, on goal setting and productivity. We must stop pretending to know everything! If you are down or depressed about life, I believe that it could be because you're focusing on the wrong things. Life is hard, yes; but it's also amazing! With your mind, you can choose to focus on things that give you a more exciting experience. A LION leader knows that in order for NEW things to reveal themselves, we must to be willing to abandon OLD perspectives that are not working.

Excitement

One of my favorite sayings is this, "Ignorance on FIRE is better than knowledge on ICE." The problem that many of us have is that we're holding so tightly to what we already know that our brains are getting bored. Excitement, on the other hand, will not only draw greatness out of you but it will also draw great people TO you.

If you're not excited about the future and what's possible, you are doomed to only want to relive the past. I like to tell people, "The glory days lead to mediocre days." Don't think about your childhood too often, your high school days, or your past relationships. Think about your future, then get excited about the people you will meet and the things you will do. Excitement is like a fire that will prompt you to take action in areas where you may be holding back. Turn up the music, paint your office, hang up some pictures, read some new books, try some new restaurants, and – *please* - get excited about what's coming. If you anticipate it, visualize it and work for it, it will happen!

The only difference between fear and excitement toward something is your attitude about it. I believe there are three types of people we need to surround ourselves with: the inspired, the grateful, and, perhaps most importantly, the excited. Commit to being someone who causes your family, your team, and your friends to be excited about the future as well.

Forgiveness

It takes a strong person to say the words, "I am sorry" and an even stronger person to forgive. Mahatma Gandhi said, "Forgiveness is the attitude of the strong." In this life, you will feel pain. People will hurt you, and you will hurt people. Yet we all have a process that we must walk through if we're hoping to grow, I believe we have matured when we realize that everything that happens to us does not necessarily deserve a response; especially not a negative one.

Elon Musk, the CEO of Tesla and SpaceX, said, "Life is too short to carry long-term grudges." When we're unwilling to forgive, we carry a load of resentment and un-forgiveness with us that we are not meant to carry. We only have so much mental and emotional capacity, and un-forgiveness can preoccupy much of both. I have heard it said that, "Forgiveness is to set a prisoner free only to realize the prisoner was yourself."

Forgiveness simply means that you care more about showing honor to yourself and someone else than you care about staying stuck. Being right sometimes keeps us stuck! When we forgive, it means we are willing to look at the part we played in the event, how it transpired, and also look for ways we can learn and improve from it.

As I shared previously, forgiveness doesn't mean that you have to forget; it simply means that you're willing to release whatever happened so that you can walk away free. When you fully understand that you actually deserve to be free, you won't hold onto un-forgiveness anymore.

Un-forgiveness gives you a sense of certainty and control, but you're attempting to control the wrong thing. When you're attempting to control the wrong thing, your focus is on the wrong things. It's the harmful emotions and perspectives you're creating in your life that cause you to continue to remain wounded. On the other hand, forgiveness softens our hearts as well as our minds to create new things and experience better feelings. Since emotion drives so much of our decisions, carrying negative emotion will often cause us to make negative choices. However, you and I deserve better, and the people we lead deserve better as well. Forgiveness is one of the best ways to lead BY EXAMPLE.

Generosity

The world of the generous gets larger and larger, while the world of the stingy gets smaller and smaller. Winston Churchill said, "We make a living by what we get, but we make a life by what we give." There are generally two types of people in the world - the givers and the takers. If we're only going to take from the planet and from its people, we're not truly LION leaders.

Some of the gifts I have given to other people have

opened the door for amazing things in return. I once gave a man a new phone, and he later gave me a new car. Now, I'm not saying that you should give away things in hopes that people will give you something better. That isn't giving; that's manipulation. When we operate with generosity, we send a message to the world that we are not thinking only of ourselves. Generosity is like a flowing stream, if the flow stops, the water becomes susceptible to bacteria and all sorts of contaminants. It was Pablo Picasso who said, "The meaning of life is to find your gift. The purpose of life is to give it away."

In business, I have heard many successful people say that we should give ourselves away to as many people as we can, so that they can't imagine doing life without us. I believe this to be very true! That doesn't mean you should lower your values so much that you don't ask for what you're worth, but you should be willing to sow your gifts and talents into the world, in order to make it better for all of us.

Giving is an expression of your soul. Being willing to part with things, is a way of saying that we believe better things can - and will - come our way. LION leaders think of their relationships as their PRIDE, which is much like a TRIBE. Not everyone will fit into your tribe, but that doesn't mean that you can't be kind and generous to them as well. Use your giving as a weapon against scarcity thinking and lack. When we give we are reminding our brain that life isn't always about what we have, it's about what we do with what we have.

***

As we get close to the end of this book, I want to remind you of what LION leadership is all about.

LION leadership is about being bold and courageous, while leaving a legacy that cannot be erased. Boldness simply means that we will stand for what we believe in, while courage means we will act, even when we are afraid. In the uncertain times that we live in, boldness and courage are needed now more than ever.

We often talk about being willing to fight for the things that we want, but many times the fight we must engage in is the one we fight in defending our core values. When we take a stand for our values, we are standing for what is right for humanity. The world is broken, and that means there are ample opportunities for LION leaders to face those challenges and become the solution. The time to stop complaining and start working has arrived.

Maybe, for you today, being BOLD means having the conversation that you know you need to have with someone. Even if your hands are shaking and your heart is pounding, do it. If you need to step away from a relationship that's not working, do it. If it's time to get your finances in order by catching up on things from your past, do it. If it's time to start honoring your body by exercising and eating properly, do it. One decision, one action, one word, one connection, can change the rest of your life forever. Do it!

In addition to being BOLD and COURAGEOUS, I also want to encourage you to SERVE. The world we are living in right now is broken - whether by greed, selfishness or just plain evil. People who do not live by the principles we've discussed in this book have made a huge negative impact on OUR world. However, we can, and we must, bring the light to the darkness.

Instead of complaining about the darkness, we need to shine our light brighter than we ever have before. We must learn to work together - putting away our insecurities, our agendas, and our ulterior motives - to simply SERVE one another. No one is going to fix this world for us. We were given this world to take care of, not to abandon. Even when others are willing to give up, we can't. If we don't give our best, who will? If we don't share the hope and the love that we have been given, who will? If we don't do the work, who will?

The excuses that we have bought and the lies that we have believed, MUST stop. I'm challenging you now, as a LION leader, to think bigger than you ever have before, and to get to work. Unplug from the mass media, turn off your TV, put down your phone and get focused. Leverage all the relationships that you have to do something bigger than you've ever done before. Unity is the key. Lions know how to stand alone, but they also stand together. Identify a few people that you would like to develop stronger relationships with, reach out to those people, share a copy of this book and begin to work together making a difference. Together you can do it.

And finally, as a LION leader, I ask that you keep the following agreements:

Never gossip

Regardless of what someone else may have said about you or done to you, do not gossip. If you notice negative things coming out of your mouth, check your heart, change your perspective, and speak life.

Always keep your word

Even in the small things, it's important to let your YES be YES, and your NO be NO. If you say you'll do something, do it. If you know you're not going to do it, don't say that you will. The more you keep your agreements, the more you will trust yourself. If you're going to lead like a LION, and become the best version of yourself, you must learn to keep your word.

Do more than is expected

Whether at work, at home, with friends, family, or business colleagues, always do more than is expected of you. Remove the words "have to" from your vocabulary. Every time you say, "I have to," you're unconsciously telling yourself that you are a victim and that you are out of control. Replace the words "have to" with the words "choose to." When you practice using this new phrase you will begin to feel more empowered and in control as you go throughout your day.

Honor yourself

Take good care of you. Watch what you eat, watch what you drink and develop a daily discipline that will keep you on track to becoming a healthier person. Remember, people hear best with their eyes, so lead by example. Don't just talk about doing the right thing, do the right thing for you and for others. When you feel better it will be easier to do better. Don't take your health for granted; it is a gift.

Remind yourself DAILY that you ARE a LION

Imam Ash-Shafi'i said, "Don't you see the lion? He's silent, and yet he is feared, while the dog barks constantly and is despised."

As you practice keeping these agreements, remember to approach your life one day at a time. We can begin to feel overwhelmed, not when we think of our future, but when we try to control it. When we get overwhelmed, thinking that there's so much for us to do, our natural response is to shut down and pull back. Remember, change doesn't happen in a day, change happens daily. To grow great fruit on a tree, the tree must develop strong roots, and strong roots always take time to grow. So don't rush the process.

As you continually grow into the leader you were

created to be, you will build the character, consistency, and integrity that you will need in order to maintain the success that will eventually come your way.

Thank you for allowing me to share these insights with you. I believe that together we are making a positive impact on our world.

***

Notes

Chapter 1

Prepare for Transition

"Life is pleasant, death is peaceful. It's the transition that is troublesome."

Isaac Asimov

Notes

Chapter 2

Watch what you believe

"99% of the decisions that you think you are making in life, you're not making. Your belief systems are making them for you."

Brian Klemmer

Notes

Chapter 3

Check your perspective

"The secret of change is to focus all of your energy not on fighting the old, but building the new."

Socrates

Notes

Chapter 4

Leave the past in the past

"It's not the mountains ahead that we have to climb that wear us out; it's simply the pebble in our shoe."

Muhammad Ali

Notes

Chapter 5

Adopt a LION mindset

"I failed my way to success."

Thomas Edison

Notes

Chapter 6

Think forward
"Our lust for comfort murders the passions of our soul."
Kahlil Gibran

Notes

Chapter 7

Dream impossible dreams

"The world is a dangerous place. Not because of those who do evil, but because of those who look on and do nothing."

Albert Einstein

Notes

Chapter 8

Be the teammate you want to have

"It was pride that changed angels to devils, and it's humility that makes men as angels."

Saint Augustine

Notes

Chapter 9

Forge LION-Level connections

"Teamwork begins with the building of trust, and the only way to do that is to overcome our need for invulnerability."

Patrick Lencioni

Notes

Chapter 10

Take ACTION
"Adversity introduces a man to himself."
Albert Einstein

Notes

Chapter 11

Lead like a LION

"Your biggest opportunity may be right here, where you are, right now."
Napoleon Hill

Ronnie Doss Companies, LLC
website: www.DossTeam.com
email: info@DossTeam.com
phone: 615-881-9431

RONNIE DOSS